THE CONTENT OF WATERCOLOR

THE CONTENT

EDWARD REEP

OF WATERCOLOR

VAN NOSTRAND REINHOLD COMPANY

NEW YORK   TORONTO   LONDON   MELBOURNE

To my wife, Pat,

to whom this book is dedicated,

my enduring gratitude not only for her valuable help

but for her patience, understanding, and encouragement.

The author is deeply indebted to the numerous artists, collectors, museums, and galleries without whose help this book would not have been possible. I wish to thank librarian Cal Davis and her staff at the Los Angeles County Art Museum, Richard Collins and his staff at the Chouinard Art School of the California Institute of the Arts, and, most particularly, Mrs. Diane Galli and Miss Blanche Nishimura for their assistance. My special thanks to Patricia Howard for her skillful research, Frederik Nieuwenhuijs for his translations, Ruth Marie Judge for her voluntary aid, and Donald Lent of the Noland Paper Corporation for his generous assistance.

Designed by Myron Hall III. Printed by Halliday Lithograph Corporation. Color printed by Mastercraft Lithographers, Inc. Bound by A. Horowitz & Son. Published by Van Nostrand Reinhold Company, 450 West 33 Street, New York, N.Y. 10001. Published simultaneously in Canada by D. Van Nostrand Company (Canada), Ltd.

CONTENTS

Foreword   7

Introduction   9

1 The Legacy of Watercolor   12

2 The Background of the Artist   38

3 The Contemporary School   58

4 The Dynamics of the Medium   78

5 A Chronology of Change   98

6 Related and Other Water-soluble Media   118

Appendix   135

Materials and Equipment   136

Bibliography   140

Index   142

FOREWORD

This is not a "how-to-do-it" or "how-I-do-it" book. It is, on the contrary, intended to be the very antithesis of such teaching; for while the exposure of personal methodology may prove entertaining, there is little else to be gained from it.

When the young artist completes his formal training, he launches a very private and often very lonely career. He may no longer depend upon textbook diagrams or classroom instruction, but must now do for himself. Personal values and meanings immediately become a vital part of his struggles and will ultimately mold his artistic character.

Max Doerner has written: "It is no more possible to learn to paint from books, than to learn to swim on a sofa." I would like to add that while you may practice your swimming stroke on that same sofa, you will eventually have to jump in the water. You may theorize, speculate, and dream, but as a painter you will ultimately have to set it down again and again. There is no short cut; there are no born geniuses!

All too often the artist is referred to as "talented," a term I thoroughly detest. Every real artist that I have known can work nine out of ten men into the ground. If his "talent" needs explanation, it is to be found in the realm of such things as dedication, perseverance, love, empathy, and belief. Some claim that they cannot draw a straight line. While I could never fully understand why they might wish to, it is altogether likely that they have never tried! Failure as well as success has to be earned.

My obligation in preparing this volume is unmistakably clear to me. It is to encourage those who would paint (especially with watercolor) to explore, investigate, and react, and not hide behind a magic success formula. To those whose work remains unchanging, I offer this as an invitation to do something about it. For others who are not painters, yet find the world of art irresistible, it is my hope that you will find *The Content of Watercolor* an edifying experience.

Standing Nude by Auguste Rodin.
Watercolor and pencil.
17½ x 12⅜ inches.

A Theatrical Character by Katsushika Hokusai. Watercolor and ink on paper. 7⁷⁄₁₆ x 10⁹⁄₁₆ inches.

INTRODUCTION

To be free in the sense of being able to make independent choices means that the free person must know a great deal, must be sensitive to a wide variety of experiences, and must have enough confidence in his own judgment to assert it and to learn how to correct it through further experience. It also means that he must have learned to respond to other people and other ideas different from his own, rather than reacting against them, and that he has learned to accept differences as natural rather than as a threat to himself and his whole style of life.

(From "Moral Values and the Experience of Art," in Art and the Intellect *by Harold Taylor,* © *1952 and 1960 by The Museum of Modern Art, New York)*

To reach the individual, bring out of him what he already knows, that is the trick! To develop sensitivities, to be aware, informed, and alert, and to persevere — from these experiences the true artist develops. Only the hapless dilettante, the sycophant or the frustrated student will ape his teacher beyond the point at which learning from another's experience is relevant. One must not force-feed one's own limitations upon others.

My purpose is to place before the reader, in word and picture, the singular beauty of the watercolor medium. It is not only vital to explain how and why watercolor is technically unique while possessing obvious limitations, but to underscore its true gift of intimate, spontaneous expression. And while it is possible to abuse a medium or tool, we encourage everyone to strain against all boundaries in the search for new and rewarding events.

Through long experience in this field as both artist and teacher, I have become increasingly aware over the years that craftsmanship is a simple result of practice. Nicolaides speaks of craftsmanship in painting as mere virtuosity and calls it a skill that may hide lack of real perception. He suggests that in the end there can be only expression. Most painters will rate content, subject matter, and technique in that order of importance. In all portions of this book you will find repeated emphasis upon these beliefs, almost to the point of redundancy; yet it is important that we take that risk.

The elaborate world of sophisticated materials will not be dealt with in the sense that there are special effects to be achieved. Nor will equipment be discussed beyond the advantage which may be gained by using versatile, quality products or by avoiding others. Here, too, we will stress *why* and not *what*. There have been too many diagrams, suggestions, and far too many rules laid down already.

Watercolor has played an enormous role in the history of art, especially in the Oriental world. This long legacy is traced in Section 1, beginning in the prehistoric era with the art of the Stone Age. These ancient cave and rock paintings were of necessity executed with a very liquid paint, and the results often resemble those of the contemporary artist at work with turpentine, acrylic or watercolor wash. For this reason alone the history of watercolor begins with extraordinary drama.

The development that follows maintains a startling pace. Cave walls and rock surfaces give way to the more refined plastered walls of the Egyptians, Greeks, Etruscans, and Romans. Egyptian scribes applied watercolor to rolls of papyrus, and the Orientals employed rice papers with unusual effect. With the Renaissance, the penmanship of the painter begins to take hold, to ultimately dominate the medium. Tonality insinuates itself and eliminates the chromatic beauty contained in the flat, bright colors of the ancients. The critics alertly label such work as "watercolor-drawing," and innocently proclaim that the medium is extremely difficult to manage. Watercolor is dubbed "the medium of the masters."

In the early 19th century the British schools virtually suffocate the medium in overemphasizing a strict methodology more closely bound to documentation than artistic expression. It remained for Turner almost single-handedly to rescue watercolor from this fate with his outpouring of vital and spontaneous work. Turner gives us our first glimpse of things to come. Toward the end of the 19th century, the French Impressionists add sparkling color-and-light experiences. Then, soon after the turn of the century, the German Expressionists and an awakening American school completely restore the status of watercolor with dynamic energy and dramatic innovation.

In Section 2, we take a brief but hard look at the artist's background, the things he painstakingly explores and the enormousness of his task. The background outlined herein is but a sample of the vast world that serious young painters explore during their years of training. We could not begin to encompass all of the areas of interest and study that concern him — studies both formal and private. With this in mind, no longer may we regard artists as merely gifted or skilled workmen, nor can the amateur, neophyte or dilettante honestly call himself a painter.

The contemporary artist is treated in a very personal way in Section 3. The text traces the contemporary school to its origins in Impressionism and Expressionism, while simultaneously looking upon the total movement as a revolt against the long tradition of Renaissance thinking. The interim schools are noted carefully, with Dada singled out as an important predecessor of contemporary art. For the most part, aside from the historical survey, living artists supply us with personal commentaries through their work and word. There has been no attempt to guide or in any way control this commentary. Understandably, this becomes the most enticing section for the author, since he too is invigorated by the persuasions of other painters.

Perhaps there is more visual excitement in Sections 4 and 6 than in the others. Wherever possible, there has been an attempt to accompany the work reproduced with an enlarged detail of the painting. This provides a most unusual optical journey for the viewer, although some of the enlargements are more revealing than others. By way of explanation, the difficulty of getting these details has been fearsome. It entailed selecting from available work, noting the section, returning the work, and praying that good results would be forthcoming. Several selections had to be abandoned simply because the negatives were no longer available, while in some instances the enlargements were sacrificed as they were thought to be unnecessary.

The preliminary text of Section 4, which is devoted to the dynamics of watercolor, pecks away at the ludicrous formula-oriented artist and offers a visual autopsy of pictorial content. There is humor involved in the text, based mostly upon the author's misfortunes as a student, when technique was demanded as an end in itself. The dynamics of watercolor are carefully explored in order to afford liberation and full expression through intelligent analysis. The desire is to breed confidence, not futility.

Moving into the media related to watercolor, such as acrylic, tempera, etc., enlargements are again employed in Section 6, with startling effect. Here, collage and impasto thicknesses appear along with the more opaque paints and suggest further dimensions. For example, it is captivating to watch Morris Louis transform an essentially opaque acrylic into a translucent symphony, or to observe the infinite variations that occur when paint and support are altered. In addition to a survey of works in the related fields of water-base paint, we are afforded a dramatic view of the artist straining against traditional barriers.

The sensitive reader will undoubtedly understand the author's concern in Section 5, the area devoted to his own paintings. All artists would like their work to speak for itself whenever possible. In this treatise, however, the text explanations help provide a far more revealing essay, and they are straightforward. In my opinion, such a written analysis can only be attempted with one's own efforts and not otherwise. Apropos, and in retrospect, some of the early work is admittedly based more upon enthusiasm than knowledge or insight. However, the chronology of work should prove illuminating and the lessons, it is hoped, clear.

If rules and regulations are ultimately to be denied and if method-approaches are deemed futile, then how might this particular book be most helpful? While the answer to such a question would prove as complex as the question itself, the following is submitted: Like most treatises, it should not be read from cover to cover and then abandoned forever. It is not an examination to be taken one day and forgotten the next. It ought to be explored with discrimination; that is to say, one thing may be used and the next spurned. Everything in this book cannot possibly help you, nor can it always be useful to you at a given time. Returning later to the very thesis that was once cast aside may prove to be most helpful. This is a source book of information that has been drawn from inspiration, and this knowledge hopefully will provide rare and exciting new painting experiences. There is so much that remains untapped and awaiting release deep within each of us that it would be lamentable not to investigate these individual worlds of discovery.

THE LEGACY

OF WATERCOLOR

In order to fully appreciate the nature of watercolor today it will serve us well to examine briefly some of its origins. While it is impossible to present a complete document of so vast a subject, we may attempt to highlight the most significant contributions and at the same time relate them to the purposes of this book.

The monumentality of this task grows when one realizes that the earliest known paintings, dating roughly 20,000 B.C., were no doubt executed in a water-base medium. Of greater import, these works look more like contemporary painting than do the efforts of the more "advanced" schools to follow, such as Chinese, Persian, or Renaissance. One has only to examine the cave-wall art of Altamira, Spain, or of Lascaux, France, to witness this astonishing revelation. By careful examination of the Bushman paintings of South Africa, and the work of the North Australian Aborigines, one gains even further reassurance. This latter work of cave-wall, rock, or bark painting will appear remarkably contemporary, almost identical to many of today's efforts.

The hunting and animal motifs which dominated early art are clearly understandable, since survival was of primary importance.

Whether these scenes had further and specific meanings is debatable, but I am inclined to agree with those scholars of paleolithic art who believe they did. For example, it appears reasonably certain that there were utilitarian demands for the numerous single animal paintings found on cave walls. Wall scars in strategic areas and other clues indicate that they were used as part of a training program for the hunter. For example, working from the single animal paintings, the young hunter could be shown where the vital striking areas existed, and evidence suggests that spears were actually driven into the paintings in practicing the kill.

Of greater pertinence for us is the fact that these works reveal a softness and spontaneity that are bound to emotion. Undoubtedly the roughness of the walls demanded a very aqueous paint in order to cover the surface, and this in turn lent itself to the artist's excitement and intensity in executing the work. The magic of this performance was quite obviously shared by both the artist and the spectator.

The greatest contributions in the history of watercolor come from the Far Eastern schools of painting. As early as the Nara Period in the eighth century,

Sumi-e painting (opposite) by Ken Wakeshima. Sumi ink on rice paper. 10 x 12 inches.

13

the Japanese executed scrolls, mainly in ink on paper, which remain extremely vibrant and spontaneous to this day. Japanese culture was strongly influenced by T'ang China at the time, and painting styles in particular were taken from Indian prototypes carried eastward through Central Asia, China, and Korea.

Whether secular or religious, Oriental art is superb in concept and execution and has remained unexcelled. Watercolor is its natural medium, for not only did the Oriental child develop exceptional dexterity through the delicate manipulation of his chopsticks, but he was virtually weaned with a brush in his hands. While it may seem incongruous, since there are 72 important laws that govern Japanese painting, the Japanese artists were masters of the subjective attitude. The viewer of the Oriental landscape senses at once that he is a part of it, or is in it and surrounded by it. It suffuses him with its overpowering sense of scale and depth. It is aromatic, mysterious, and adventuresome. The sheer beauty of the work gives the viewer a heady experience. Contrast this with the traditional European concept in which the viewer stands apart from the painting. It was something to be viewed, to witness, as if it were some sort of occurrence participated in by others. Not until the French Impressionists was there a major change in this point of view, and with it a recognition of the true contribution of Eastern art. For along with it came an understanding of the flattened patterns, the chroma, and the use of graphic symbols, plus the art of selection, elimination, or the *unsaid.*

Nowhere in the history of painting has the medium of pure, essentially transparent watercolor been relied upon more exclusively than in Oriental art. The school of *Sumi e* (black picture), while limited to black and white, depends entirely upon the subtle nuances of tonal wash gradations. These tones are produced from a cake of black color, which resembles the hard-pan watercolors used in our elementary schools. The results are exceptionally spontaneous since overworking is frowned upon.

The laws that govern *Sumi e* painting are far too numerous to recount here, but one may not take the name of the *Sumi* master until all the strict teachings have been absorbed. One such law is called *fude no chikara,* which means "the strength of the brush stroke." While the contemporary painter might feel limited working under imposed restrictions and rules, this is not so with *fude no chikara.* Conversely, under this law, at the precise moment of paint application to surface, the artist's sentiment or feeling must be transmitted from within, through his arm and hand, through the brush, and onto the painting surface. His sense of the vital forces of power, restraint, fragility, softness, or harshness continues to pour steadily into his work until completion.

We may compare the results of *fude no chikara* with those of the contemporary action painter, or find a strong resemblance to the older school of *alla prima* painting. *Alla prima* painting, popularly known as wet-into-wet or to-be-completed-at-one-sitting, I prefer to explain as "that which begins with emotion and ends with emotion." The lessons contained in *fude no chikara* were so completely lacking in the work of the English, French, Italian, and American painters (especially those working in watercolor), that their paintings were often tired, worn, and limp by comparison. We find to this day this saccharine and flabby work being produced and espoused.

Tempera painting dominated the world of the ancients and may be classified technically as a form of watercolor. But there is far deeper meaning to be found here than in mere definition, despite the fact that free-flowing line and an abundance of glazing were prevalent. For example, the artists of Egypt, or scribes as they were called, were required in apprenticeship to execute their work on papyrus rolls, which encouraged quickness and fluidity. This influence is readily noted in their wall paintings (usually in tombs), for despite the specific demands of a craft handed down from one generation to another, individual and expressive characteristics are felt. It must be kept in mind that the art of the scribe was primarily concerned with death. Tomb decorations were dominated by the need to provide for the life after death of important or wealthy persons. His subjects were ritualistic, biographical, or mythological, and included graphic symbols and hieroglyphics. There was no attempt to portray literally nature or people, yet the results were extremely realistic. This delicate paradox is readily understood when one recognizes the mastery of expression, pattern, and flat, bright color that dominates Egyptian painting and produces an inimitable timelessness.

The Etruscans, on the other hand, being highly influenced by the Orientals, presented an even livelier version of tomb paintings. They decorated their walls, ceilings, terra-cotta slabs, urns and sarcophagi with scenes of people, animals, and plants. All of this, as in Egyptian art, was prepared mainly to document the life of the deceased and/or to record his funerary rites. Although the Etruscans were strong admirers of the Greeks, they were unable to compete with the Greek mastery of draftsmanship.

A later record of Italian painting is to be found in the art of the Romans, which has endured remarkably well. Relying essentially on tempera along with very careful preparation of the ground support, the Roman artist-craftsman became even more sophisticated by adding a wax-encaustic element to his paint when exposure problems were present. It is small wonder that Roman art has remained in excellent condition to this day, for those two concerns of ground and pigment are of prime import to all artists.

The Roman artist was involved with the recording of historical events, military conquests, and honorific rites. He presented them in amazingly illusionistic landscape settings, in addition to producing isolated landscapes, garden scenes, and even still-lifes. Modest and elaborate homes alike were profusely decorated, as evidenced by the excavations of Pompeii. Walls, ceilings, floors, furniture — indeed everything was painted with color that served to provide spiritual and emotional meanings in addition to decorative values. *Brushless* areas were played against translucent line on pale off-white surfaces that produced delicate sensations. Then, too, a precise *absence of color* was employed for similar purposes of achieving special meaning. For example, a room might be done in a startling black and white theme, which is a most contemporary attitude. While there was a very definite striving for form through the use of light and shade, it is noteworthy that this period produced innovations through analysis of light that suggest future impressionistic thinking.

So when we think of the legacy of watercolor we are irresistibly directed to the magnificence of Ancient and Eastern art, for these worlds of art, while highly developed for their time, were not concerned with labels of media. Yet with all of the restrictions of technique and style, plus utilitarian demands, there remains a strong flavor of magic and discovery, remarkably direct.

Turning to the Middle Ages, watercolor as such, with the possible exception of some fantastically rewarding frescoes, was ignored. Stones and metals invaded the art form, and decoration became a chief concern. The Byzantines stunned the world of art with overpowering mosaics, and the superb stained-glass windows of the Middle Ages played a vital role in influencing the general art mold. Manuscripts, tapestries, and miniatures (notably Persian), preoccupied artists, and produced lasting influences. Religious themes dominated the masterworks of Giotto, Duccio, and Lorenzetti; while Bosch and Van Eyck dazzled all with incredible fantasies.

However, it remained for the artists of the Renaissance to revive watercolor and establish a sound base for its future role as a major painting medium. For here, primarily through preliminary sketches, we sense the awakening of the intimate world of the artist through his penmanship.

Watercolor became an inexorable part of drawing, and was to become classified as such. This regrettable and somewhat naive pattern is still held to faithfully by various critics and art historians who either cannot detect differences or who enjoy artistic snobbery. For to refer to an oil painting as painting, and to a watercolor painting as a drawing is pure foolishness. Yet in all fairness there was cause for this attitude during the Renaissance period.

Dürer brought watercolor to a new plateau, and the works of Rembrandt and Tiepolo were destined to reacquaint artists with the singular beauty of the spontaneous statement. Through watercolor, painters were struck with the rare opportunity to gain freedom and achieve rapidly. Their preparation work alone displayed emotional involvement heretofore unknown, except perhaps in the aforementioned Oriental world.

Until we come to the English school, headed by Blake and Turner, there is little to note. This may seem paradoxical, for surely here lay the very foundation of contemporary watercolor as a major medium. But this was due to a host of reasons, not the least of which was the enormous interest in watercolor and the copious amount of work devoted exclusively to the medium. It is unfortunate that while the artists working with watercolor at that time were dedicated and excited about their efforts, retrospection offers up little more than ennui.

It is noteworthy that the beginning of the "watercolor society" or "club" as we know it today, dates back to this precise era, as these early 19th century English artists reacted to the snubbing of their work in watercolor. They felt that their watercolors were being given second-class consideration, and they had the evidence to support their claims. The best oil paintings were always hung in the main gallery of an exhibition, whereas the watercolors were automatically lumped together with the inferior oils in adjoining rooms. This prompted them to form societies for the exclusive exhibition of watercolors. This practice not only spread but has continued to this day.

The singular contributions of Turner have proved meaningful and enduring; yet it is odd that the bulk of his watercolors were painted on landscape locations as a preparation for later and more ambitious oils. While Turner's oils were greatly enhanced by this procedure, it remained for his sketches in watercolor to capture an essence and brilliance which placed him far beyond his contemporaries. When we contrast his work with that of Paul Sandby, a mannerist, romantic painter of the eighteenth century, we clearly feel the tedious preoccupation with overembellishment, so popular at the time.

In America, during the latter half of the nineteenth century, Winslow Homer brought a new meaning to the medium. His now classic Bahamian series stood apart as the epitome of freshness and vitality. His work offers a wide sensory appeal as one inhales sea air, stands against the wind, or cuts through tropical flora. Prendergast and Demuth added new dimensions to Homer's work; while their work was of a less rugged nature, both men were superb composers and draftsmen. Now, into the twentieth century, Davies, Feininger, and a whole new school including Marin and Burchfield brought watercolor in America to a resplendent level.

It is amusing and significant to note that Homer attached far more importance to his watercolors than to his oils. At the Pan American Exposition Exhibition in Buffalo at the turn of the century, Homer insisted that his watercolors, not his oils, represented him. Time has given generous support to Homer's wisdom.

The French Impressionists and German Expressionists concurrently were creating separate and dramatic paintings of their own with watercolor. Reacting with vigor against tradition in general and the Renaissance in particular, it is obvious that their efforts remain largely responsible for the complexion of today's art scene. Caught up in the excitement and discoveries of the day, watercolor emerged not only as a spontaneous medium, but as in the work of Paul Cézanne, an enigmatic, solidly structured, yet transparent medium as well. Through Cézanne's dedication to the re-creation of light, plus the requirement that the viewer *reassemble* the work, he became known as the "great innovator." If ever there was a need to support the old cliche that "watercolor is the medium of the masters," we need only point to Cézanne and his genius in composition.

The Expressionists brought a new color dimension to all of painting, including watercolor. Their efforts simply exploded from the walls and poured forth dazzling groupings of colors. Totally subjective, and purposely ignoring all past lessons of light and shade, their work hinted of things to come. The theory of kinetic or *inner* energy was exploited, and art horizons immediately widened. Paul Klee and Wassily Kandinsky brought enormous intellect and wit to their art, while Nolde followed with an outpouring of small, brilliantly colored works.

The lessons had been learned, and now they were being abandoned. The cave-wall paintings formed a beginning, the Renaissance a high point, and Cézanne's impressionism heralded a counter-reaction to all that had gone before. The horizons of painting widened to establish a broader plateau that would, hopefully, support the imminent creative explosion to follow. There would be newer lessons but they were not yet clearly in view; however, what of the old? In the next section we will carefully examine the fundamental needs of the contemporary painter, which are based in great part upon his monumental legacy.

Lascaux Cave (below). The great frieze on the left wall of the "Hall of Bulls."

Large Eland and Human Figures (opposite). Rock painting from Khotsa Cave, Basutoland, South African Union.

This extraordinary wall painting from the Lascaux Caves begins our pictorial survey of the legacy of watercolor. It is unquestionably a remarkable work from the standpoint of durability alone; but in view of the technical restrictions imposed by surface and materials, it becomes a staggering accomplishment.

Both the Lascaux frieze and the South African rock painting opposite set the stage for our exploration of the fluid characteristic of all water-base media. The precise components of primitive painting media are of little concern to us, but we do wish to impress upon the reader the cave painter's fundamental need for an extremely liquid paint, a need dictated by the porosity of his stone and wall surfaces.

The total effect of this Paleolithic work is strikingly similar to that of the great Oriental schools to follow. Even more surprising is the marked resemblance to many contemporary works. The softness of mass, the crispness of calligraphy, the glazing of color over color and color over raw surface are methods found in today's painting. Furthermore, we may observe in "Hall of Bulls" a most impressive example of the use of the convolutions of the natural rock surface to enhance or achieve a goal. This may be likened to the inventiveness of the contemporary artist in preparing varieties of grounds and supports.

In the later Paleolithic period, or the last Ice Age, prehistoric art came into being. The rock painting shown here, from the South African Union, is the product of a culture with a highly sophisticated tradition in art. This superb example of animal and human figures, rarely superimposed, is typical of the work which was usually done in polychrome layers. Again we discover a compatibility with the historical schools or watercolor to follow.

While all primitive art is representational, it by no means could be termed realistic. Animals dominated painting, since hunting was a chief concern, but there were paintings of processionals, rituals, and dances in which human figures would appear with animal heads. Of more pertinence to us is the rare compositional gesture and draftsmanship seen here. Scale and buoyancy are handled with such distinction that one must assume that esthetic goals were uppermost in the mind of the artist. There can be little doubt that early art was highly sophisticated.

COLLECTION OF FROBENIUS INSTITUTE, GERMANY (COURTESY OF THE MUSEUM OF MODERN ART, NEW YORK).

Fowling Scene, from a Theban tomb. 1570-1349 B.C.

This exquisite example of Egyptian painting comes from the "Empire" period of her history and is significant for several reasons. Until this dynasty (XVIII), painting had been primarily a means of decorating the stone relief of architecture and sculpture; rarely did it exist as an independent art. Because of the difficulty of carving on very coarse walls, Egyptian painters were called upon to produce prolific tomb paintings.

Still reflecting such conventions as profiling the human figure, *Fowling Scene* exhibits masterly draftsmanship and sense of design in the birds, hunting cat, and papyrus. Flat colors were mixed with gum and applied to dry plaster or stucco surfaces. Gum arabic is used to this day in confecting watercolor. In this painting, an Egyptian noble, his wife, and his daughter are depicted ridding their papyrus swamp of birds. Despite its age of well over 3,000 years, the painting still shows a most delicate application of soft glaze at work in the papyrus, birds, cat, and fish.

20

Danzatore, detail from the Tomb of the Old Man, Tarquinia, Italy. VI century B.C.

While volumes have been devoted to Etruscan Art, we are concerned only with a sample of the era in order to touch on an important step of our legacy. The remarkable Etruscan tomb frescoes not only afford us an opportunity to observe Etruscan culture and daily life, but allow us a further examination of their art itself. The Etruscan dancer shown here has been selected primarily to give an intimate view of surface and paint application.

In the main text we referred to Etruscan tomb paintings as the liveliest version of that ancient art. This was obviously due to the distracting and constant civil wars during this period, which undoubtedly arrested cultural development. The result was a bolder and less sophisticated draftsmanship applied to a cruder working surface; and the scenes reflected the Etruscans' violent preoccupation with forceful animation. The Etruscan artist plunged fearlessly into his work, decorated virtually every surface in sight, and in great measure paved the way for much of the splendid Roman art to follow.

In *Danzatore,* we note the profiling seen in the three Egyptian figures on the opposite page; yet the action is far more vigorous and there is less of a reliance upon symbolism. This comparison holds true not only with these examples, but with most Etruscan and Egyptian works. The deterioration shows clearly how the wall surface was prepared, and gives us a glimpse of the rough surface and its subsequent paint layers. We may also compare·the bold Etruscan line with its careful Egyptian counterpart. From a purely technical standpoint, a rougher surface would demand a more liquid paint, or the result would be a skipping, drier wash or line. Furthermore, in fresco painting, because the artist works on fresh plaster, control is a vital factor. A mistake often demands removal of the old plaster and re-surfacing. This alone makes such early art all the more impressive and relates it to the expanded world of watercolor to follow, in which mistakes are obviously more difficult to deal with than in traditional opaque media.

Clear Weather in the Valley. Landscape scroll (section) by Tung Yüan. Sung Dynasty (XII century?). Ink and slight color on paper.

This handsome section of a very early Chinese handscroll is attributed to the Sung Dynasty, although there has been much debate among historians in attempting to identify accurately both artist and school. Our purposes may happily ignore this controversy, and instead look to the superb performance of ink monochrome, subtlety of color gradation, and richness of total orchestration.

The origin of the watercolor medium is felt here. The inimitable qualities of the controlled accident, so vital in many phases of contemporary expression, combines with the wondrous calligraphy of the Oriental artist, the virtual innovator of the landscape painting. We are invited to explore valleys and coves, walk down mysterious pathways, and peer into detailed clusters of plant and rock formation. The magnitude and quality of early Oriental painting is a direct result of thorough training and subjective analysis.

Handscroll (detail). Yūzū Nembutsu Engi. Kamakura period, Yamatoe school. 1329. Ink, color, and gold on paper. 11$\frac{7}{16}$ x 5$\frac{5}{8}$ inches.

The exquisite handscroll shown here is one of countless works produced during the twelfth to fourteenth centuries in Japan which display superb draftsmanship and compositional control. The great tradition of drawing excellence established by the Yamatoe school is clearly evident here. These artists placed so much emphasis upon drawing that their work was often outlined first, and later filled in with color.

While this approach would be frowned upon by contemporary artists as seeming to deny all spontaneity, it is surprising how much flow and movement have been maintained. Executed in ink, color, and gold on paper, this handscroll, like others of the Yūzū Nembutsu belief, illustrates stories and incidents related to their sect. Despite the strong demands of method and subject, if one examines the line, the trees in the upper portion, and the soft gradations of color throughout, he will become aware of an amazing freedom within the self-imposed limitations.

23

View of Arco by Albrecht Dürer (1471-1528). 1495. Watercolor and gouache. 8⅞ x 8⅞ inches.

At the age of 24, Albrecht Dürer painted several landscapes in watercolor which were revolutionary in scope. Nature never had been presented with such a peculiar blending of sharp detail and atmospheric grandeur. While the Orientals were masters of the subjective landscape, it took Dürer to free European painting from ancient religious dogma and build new foundations for contemporary thinking.

This was not a new experience for Albrecht Dürer, for when only 13 he was producing self-portraits, a rare subject for any artist at the time. He later turned to animals, portraits, landscapes, and altar pieces; he worked with oil, watercolor, and pen and ink, and produced magnificent woodcuts and engravings. At the dawn of the Renaissance in Germany, Dürer unquestionably laid cornerstones for the great schools to follow.

View of Arco was painted on his return trip from Italy in 1495. It appears to capture an infinite distance that plays against the closeness of forbidding cliffs. It lives as the very essence of the ancient Italian landscape. Its awesome sense of scale is given emphasis by the nestling of walls, fortresses, and other smaller structures against the majestic mountain.

Dürer's accomplishments cannot be summed up in a single painting or even in an entire volume. His prodigious accomplishment went far beyond art; he wrote treatises on many subjects, including fortifications, proportions, and measurement. Although his greatest influence has been felt in the field of graphic art, we cannot overlook his monumental gift to the watercolor painter.

24

View of London by Rembrandt van Ryn (1606-1669). 1640. Pen, bistre, and wash. 6½ x 12½ inches.

Le Tibre en Amont de Rome by Claude Lorrain (1600-1682). Brush and bistre wash on white paper. 4¼ x 10⅝ inches.

These two significant paintings by Rembrandt and Claude Lorrain are similar in that they are both panoramic; but they are quite different in treatment. For one thing, Rembrandt's view of the London countryside, with St. Paul's in the distance, is a spontaneous, flattened, and linear experience. Executed in pen and bistre (a brown pigment made from charred wood), it deals magnificently with light and haze in essentially a monochromatic key. Lorrain, on the other hand, presents a fullness of wash and suggests an intense color contrast and reflection of light off the Tiber.

So much has been written of these famous painters, and most especially of Rembrandt, that this brief commentary could add little biographically. My purpose in showing these two works together is not only to encourage comparative viewing, but to set the stage for the unusual development of the British school which follows. Keep in mind that we have now reached a high point of spontaneous expression, and that watercolor was curiously referred to as the medium of the masters.

A Prospect of S.t Peter's Port and Castle Cornett in the Island of Guernsey.

St. Peter's Port and Castle Cornett by Thomas Phillips (1635?-1693). 1680. Ink line and watercolor. 17⅞ x 41⅛ inches.

An Ancient Beech Tree by Paul Sandby (1725-1809). 1794. Body colors (watercolor gouache). 27⅝ x 41⅝ inches.

No survey would be complete without touching upon the odd turning of the English school. For here, well over a century after the expressive vitality of Rembrandt and the chiaroscuro of Lorrain, we sink back into a world inundated with genre painting. Phillips' work is hardly classifiable as a painting. It is truly the forerunner of the architectural rendering as we know it today, and was referred to then as a platte painting. These plattes, or plot-plans, were normally drawn out in monochrome, but with the tremendous interest in watercolor at that time, Phillips added transparent color washes to his platte to increase its effectiveness.

Meanwhile, Sandby and others were contributing little more than enormous portfolios of highly romantic, idealistic and mannered works. Interest in the medium was so high at this time that clubs and societies were formed for the sole purpose of exhibiting watercolor paintings.

Ship and Cutter by J. M. W. Turner (1775-1851). Watercolor and pencil on paper. 9⅜ x 11⅜ inches.

A simple comparison of this painting with those on the opposite page will accomplish more than these words. For Joseph Mallord William Turner gave the English school a needed transfusion of vitality. *Ship and Cutter,* as a single statement, can hardly be expected to display the fullness of his total contribution, but there can be no questioning its message.

Turner's watercolors are essentially studies for his oils or mezzotints, but they are obviously filled with more emotional content than the more elaborate works to follow. He peered long and hard into nature, searching for an internal truth rather than the customary outer veneer. His early training as a draftsman — he was selling his drawings at the age of 12 — no doubt endowed him with the necessary confidence to work with rare enthusiasm in the outdoor world he loved.

It is not difficult to understand that this brash upstart was not readily accepted by his fellow members of the Royal Academy, for his innovations posed a serious challenge to their traditions. Nor is it surprising to note that Turner's idol, the man he tried to emulate, was Claude Lorrain. We have seen the drama of Lorrain, which must have moved Turner; but never before had the painting world experienced such a dynamic and tempestuous brush as that wielded by Turner. While others were relying upon subject matter alone, Turner displays in *Ship and Cutter* an innovative spirit that provides ammunition for those who contend that he was the father of the contemporary school. He lets slashing brush strokes, spattered paint, and unfinished wash support his perilous theme. He controls conflicting diagonals masterfully with a superb disorder of things coming undone, in motion and transit, all struggling for survival.

The Whirlwind of Lovers (Hell, Canto 5) by William Blake (1757-1827). Ink line and watercolor. 14½ x 20½ inches.

Because of Turner's enormous impact upon the art world, we have purposely placed him before William Blake in order to play Turner against his flaccid predecessors. It is of little consequence that our chronology suffers a slight shock, for at best Blake can hardly be placed into any normal sequence of art events.

William Blake was unique: there will never be another like him. He was hardly a painter in the accepted sense, although he used watercolor almost exclusively to carry out his visionary works. These were often illustrations for his own poetic writings and those of the Bible. He composed with his imagination, ignored convention, and held fast to his own subjective goals.

The Whirlwind of Lovers is but one of a prolific outpouring of magnetic works which powerfully attest to this great man's burning personality. We look for no technical guidance or classic draftsmanship here, yet William Blake, by virtue of his imagination and vision, is one of the great painters of all time.

Slope of a Hill by Eugene Delacroix (1798-1863). Watercolor on paper.

The most notable painter and the leading figure of the romantic movement in France, Delacroix presents us with the antithesis of the Blake on the opposite page. Fresh, spontaneous, and spatial, brilliant in panoramic scale, *Slope of a Hill* is unlike even Delacroix's own carefully planned oils. But despite this sparkling, breezy jacket, there is a careful transposing of light and dark masses in the lower portion of the painting. This must be the result of Delacroix's studies under Gros and his admiration for Gericault, Rubens, and Veronese, all classically involved with subject and form.

While his output was prodigious, his most satisfying works remain his colorful sketches, drawings, and watercolor paintings.

Man Reading in a Garden by Honoré Daumier (1808-1879). 1854-56. Wash drawing on paper. $13^{15}/_{16}$ x $10^{5}/_{8}$ inches.

Once again we witness a classic control of form and structure in this amazingly solid performance by Daumier. Still, there is a premonition in this work of impressionist things to come. The loose brush and line, and the patient love for intense contrasts that characterize Daumier's work, are clearly evident. Originally a cartoonist, he eventually completed over 4,000 lithographs which, for the most part, furiously attack corruption and evil. His satirical and often bitter commentaries aimed at the French society around him are without parallel.

The Shell Heap by Winslow Homer (1836-1910.) 1904. Watercolor. $19\frac{11}{16}$ x 14 inches.

Nassau by Winslow Homer. 1899. Watercolor. 15 x $21\frac{3}{8}$ inches.

Winslow Homer was the first in a long line of American artists to receive wide acclaim for his watercolor efforts. Yet only recently have critics hopped on his bandwagon to speak of his modernity. They now proffer reasons why his tightly formed oils present "minimal" experiences of deepest and most profound implication. But the truth is that Homer was an illustrator, self-taught, and was happiest when cutting away from the shackles of his past. He openly felt that his watercolors were far more meaningful than his oils.

In both of the paintings shown here we share Homer's love for the open, windswept Bahama coast. His superb control of draftsmanship and structure understandably echoes his disciplined past, but there is ease and assurance in his adroit handling of the medium as well. Unquestionably Homer is the bellwether of American watercolor enthusiasts; but it is unfortunate that his work is more often emulated in method than in subjective spirit.

Low Tide, Beachmont by Maurice Brazil Prendergast (1859-1924). 1897. Pencil and watercolor on paper. 19½ x 22⅛ inches.

Simplon Pass, Avalanche Track by John Singer Sargent (1856-1925). 1911. Watercolor. 13 x 20½ inches.

The comparative essay of Prendergast and Sargent serves us with moving clarity, for time has reversed the positions of each painter. The struggling Prendergast paint- ed with little acceptance, yet is now ac- knowledged to be America's first modern painter, 50 years ahead of his time. On the other hand, Sargent's every effort was eagerly snapped up as he gained notoriety and fortune. He was a master of the ac- cepted style, a virtual pedaling-backwards when you think of Turner or Delacroix. While his virtuosity was conspicuous and unexcelled, he had little to say.

Maurice Prendergast once noted, "The love you liberate in your work is the only love you keep." His paintings gave full affirmation to his words. Watercolor for Prendergast was only a means to an end, as all media should be. He wove a pattern of beautiful people, gaily attired, happy at play; and his patchwork of color was de- voted to the re-establishment of nature as he saw and loved it. He dabbed at his sur- face with an awkward, halting brush, and made convenient rules as he went. No- where do paintings more richly endorse the content of watercolor.

31

Two Prostitutes by Georges Rouault (1871-1958). 1906. Watercolor. 26½ x 22¼ inches.

An overpowering statement, *Two Prostitutes* stands as a giant step forward in the history of watercolor painting. Rouault unleashes all of his disgust for vice and corruption in depicting these pitiful, grotesque creatures; and yet he does so with an underlying empathy of majestic proportion.

A student of Gustave Moreau, Rouault had already completed his apprenticeship to a stained-glass window maker when he enrolled at the Ecole des Beaux-Arts. Here he met Matisse, and by 1902 was associated with the Fauves. The point of this brief biographical examination is that his later work was to be greatly affected by these early events.

A deeply religious man, Rouault's initial efforts took deadly aim at a complacent, hypocritical society, largely through his commentaries on clowns, judges, and the prostitutes shown here. *Two Prostitutes*

illustrates the spontaneous potential of watercolor when employed by a powerful draftsman of profound belief. Later in life he turned directly to Biblical subject matter in order to further express his devout attitudes; and only on rare occasion did he stray from the themes of religion, landscape, and the flower still-life. Regardless of subject, Georges Rouault brought a new dimension to painting, one that fused a classic background with Fauvist overtones and the simplicity of stained glass.

Bathing Women by Raoul Dufy (1877-1953). 1920. Watercolor gouache.

Dufy, like Rouault, was classically trained, influenced to an even greater extent by the Fauvist movement and Matisse; but, additionally, he felt a kinship with Japanese draftsmanship and concepts. He abandoned all attempts at imitation at the very outset of his career and sought to express himself with bright color masses held within a design format. He gave a new life to each element, whether object or person, that entered his work. Each element found its own place in a color tempo that was singularly Dufy's. As with Prendergast, Dufy's world abounded with a *joie de vivre* that included the recording of regattas, symphonies, and the pageantry of historical events.

Whether one believes that Dufy had more philosophical goals in mind or not, we are assured that he was drawn to the abundant life. *Bathing Women* may be nothing more than three opulent ladies languidly posing for us, or it might be symbolic of far deeper meaning and implication. While all this is highly debatable, there is no question as to his devices. When Dufy paints a shape, color, or tone, he does so with resolution. He relinquishes traditional draftsmanship and reconstructs with a flowing line that animates his forms. He delights us with his innovations, and again, not unlike Prendergast, makes watercolor traditions submit to his personal goals.

33

Twittering Machine by Paul Klee (1879-1940). 1922. Watercolor, pen and ink. 16¼ x 12 inches.

The vital contribution of Paul Klee to contemporary art is almost as well documented as that of Cézanne and Picasso. His influence is felt through both his paintings and philosophical essays. Klee's *Pedagogical Sketchbook,* which was actually a plan for theoretical instruction at the Bauhaus, is still a most deserved best-seller. In essence, it contains his inductive exploration of proportionate line and structure, dimension and balance, gravitational curve, and kinetic and chromatic energy.

Klee felt it essential that the artist communicate with nature, and that, indeed, he was a part of nature. Along with his Bauhaus colleague, Wassily Kandinsky, he was dedicated to the exploration of spiritual realities rather than to the traditional, analytical approach. *Twittering Machine* is a superb example of such thinking, for there never were living birds that resembled Klee's. Yet we cannot dispute the fact that they are birds, for we are even allowed to listen to their music. If we really care to hear more, we simply turn the crank, and who knows what further songs they will sing!

Klee rarely worked large; anything over 30 inches is considered unusual. Coupled with the fact that much of his work was executed in transparent watercolor, de-

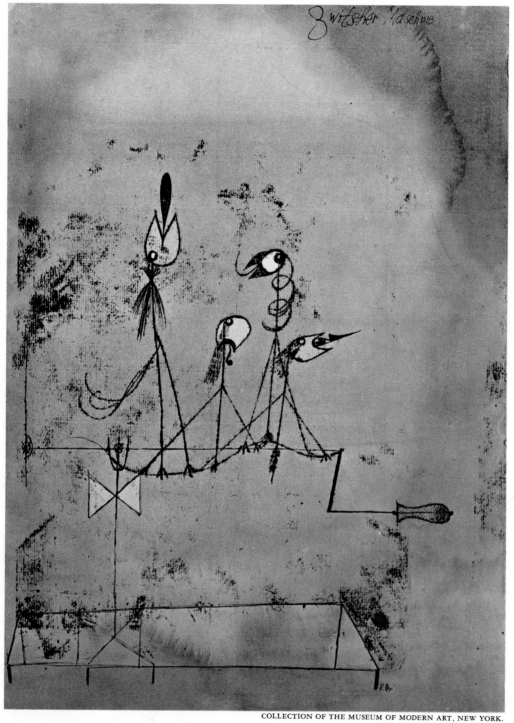

tractors allude to the slightness of his efforts. This simply brings into clear focus the utter nonsense of such empirical criticism, for if ever there was an artist in full control of his work, it was Paul Klee. He dominated his painting completely and was unerring in his choice of sign or symbol language. He intuitively depended upon the controlled accident, so generously available with watercolor, in order to disguise his preciseness and to lend counterpoise. Klee's oils, by comparison, often self-consciously struggle to attain this quality.

Twittering Machine dramatically underscores for us the formation of the contemporary school. It symbolizes the fusing of myriad heroic but scattered attempts to break away from Renaissance thinking, and presages a future art world full of new expression, invention, and discovery.

Nude Female Reclining by Egon Schiele (1890-1918). 1917. Pencil and watercolor. 11⅞ x 18⅜ inches.

A contemporary of Kokoschka and Gustav Klimt (his teacher), Schiele is regarded today as a charter member of Austrian expressionism. His work reflects a brief, turbulent life. Quitting school, he was later imprisoned on charges of producing pornographic paintings. Days after his marriage, he was conscripted for military service; and three years later he and his wife died of Spanish influenza.

Schiele's prowess as a draftsman remains unexcelled. *Nude Female Reclining* characterizes the compassion he held for the female form; it is not as violent or distorted as many of his other works. He compressed, distended, and foreshortened the figure at will, exposed joints, and developed his own symbolism. His color was off-beat, as his unruly brush scumbled its way over a tortured surface. Painted almost exclusively in watercolor, Schiele's soulful outpourings are totally dependent upon his peerless draftsmanship.

Sun Storm by Oscar Florianus Bluemner (1867-1938). 1927. Watercolor. 10 x 13¼ inches.

Relatively little is known of Oscar Bluemner, yet his wondrous *Sun Storm,* painted in 1927, will live forever. It is a most inventive, personal expression of celestial energy, one that bares a mysterious, kinetic happening.

For 16 years, before turning to painting, Bluemner worked as an architect. Trained in Germany at the Academy of Fine Arts in Berlin, he came to America in 1892, where he became a pioneer of the modern art movement.

Sun Storm is typical of Bluemner's ability to simplify form and eliminate the unessential. Of special meaning to us is the manner in which he has ordered transparent glazes of watercolor to carry out his explosive message. All too often we hear empirical utterances that insist upon spontaneity in watercolor, yet neither Egon Schiele nor Bluemner seem to heed this advice. Antithetically, the crux of Bluemner's individuality rests largely upon his determination to solidify form and structure and ignore technical considerations.

Seascape by John Marin (1870-1953). 1914. Watercolor on paper. 14 x 16 inches.

Since we rely upon John Marin's dynamic orchestration in the following section, this eloquent statement is offered more as a commitment to our chronology than to his importance in American painting. *Seascape* is a relatively serene example of the rugged genius of Marin; in 1914, when it was painted, he had not yet been moved by the Armory Show, which was to have a great effect upon him. But there is evidence in the lower portion of *Seascape* of bolder things to come. Unquestionably the name of John Marin and American watercolor painting are synonymous.

Mid-Manhattan by Lyonel Feininger (1871-1956). Pen and ink and watercolor. 40 x 56 inches.

In this single distinctive work we are immediately impressed by Feininger's passion for space and dimension. Everything he touched was fully orchestrated into a geometric network of shapes and planes: ships, buildings, people, land, and sea. Cartoonist, composer, Bauhaus professor, and an original member of the "Blue Four," Feininger's individuality and broad scope leave to us an unparalleled document.

Sun and Rocks by Charles Burchfield (1893-1967). 1950. Watercolor. 40 x 56 inches.

If Marin and American watercolor are synonymous, then Charles Burchfield and American watercolor are almost equally so. His early paintings of the sound and smell of nature are deeply moving works endowed with mystical grandeur. He loved the world of growing things, of radiant light and murky depths, which fill his work with impelling mystery. In *Sun and Rocks* we are transfixed by the mighty sun-star, as the earth submits to its furious power. Burchfield tells us of swollen, gaping, reaching, and broken forms of living and dead things, and he does this with a powerful brush that defies convention. Perhaps Charles Burchfield's secret was revealed when he noted, "I do not wander the woods free of superstition any more."

37

THE BACKGROUND

Studio per la Battaglia di Anghiari, Venice Academy, from the volume *Leonardo da Vinci.*

OF THE ARTIST

A "primitive" artist in today's society has to be either one of two things: naive or insane — unless, of course, he were to be found in some remote, secluded area. A so-called primitive living in an urban area is a pathetic figure, since he is surrounded by libraries, schools, art galleries, museums, and other artists.

In other words, there are things to be learned. How deeply involved an individual artist becomes in this learning process is a very personal matter, and where it may lead him is highly unpredictable. It may safely be said that an artist will learn in order to discard or avoid. For example, mastering perspective (a relatively simple matter) is necessary in order either to capitalize upon it or avoid it.

Several years ago a former student of mine went off to a summer of study with a renowned artist-teacher. When he returned, highly enthusiastic and bubbling over, I asked him what he had learned. "It was wonderful," he replied. "The first thing my professor told me to do was to forget about perspective!" In this instance the professor's advice was sound, as the student was well trained. But could we advise all students to do the same? Or, to rephrase it, how do you forget something you don't know?

Perspective is hardly a major course of study in any school of art today, yet the above may well be applied to all of the learning areas. The mastery of draftsmanship, picture structure, and color, plus a working knowledge of the properties of paint and support, can be no less vital to the serious painter. Nor can we begin to list the myriad explorations and penetrating studies which can prove deeply personal.

The purpose in outlining this background is not to frighten off the aspiring painter, but rather to lay it out clearly for those who are interested in painting or in becoming artists. It is essential to do this, for there are no shortcuts and there is no magic formula. Furthermore, painting is more than a craft or a skill, and it is high time to underscore this obvious truth in the area of watercolor study.

There are still other requirements apart from the formal study areas. Awareness, empathy, and integrity must play a vital role in the life of the artist; yet it is doubtful if these things can be taught beyond a point. To learn to paint is time-consuming, and one must not only persevere but learn to cope with disaster. Self-discipline is a basic requirement and must be cultivated if it is not already a part of the aspiring painter. Eventually, through the development of work habits, the tedious and strenuous task can become joyful. I stress *strenuous* because, unbeknownst to many, painting is a tremendously enervating experience.

So many of today's young artists are in search of "instant" art or "instant" success; they are of the *now* generation. Yet Joyce Cary states that "Without education, it is not possible for a man even to appreciate any art." Kandinsky, among other things, was an attorney and had a thorough education before enrolling in art school, while Giacometti was well into his thirties before holding his first one-man show.

Only when the experience of learning finally awakens, strengthens, and frees the student will he become aware of the value of his labors. The subtle indications of growing competency or sureness achieved largely through repetition and practice are reassuring and beckon one toward that golden moment when he will paint without being conscious of the act itself.

In Henri Matisse's letter to Henry Clifford, Curator of Paintings of the Philadelphia Museum, he very eloquently states the following:

I have always tried to hide my own efforts and wished my work to have the lightness and joyousness of a springtime which never lets anyone suspect the labors it has cost. So I am afraid the young, seeing in my work only the *apparent* facility and negligence in drawing, will use this as an excuse for dispensing with certain efforts which I believe necessary. The few exhibitions I have had the opportunity of seeing during these last years make me fear that young painters are avoiding the *slow* and *painful preparation* which is necessary for the education of any contemporary painter who claims to construct by color alone.

While any course of study may look naked and exposed when it is examined in its written form, I believe that so much misinformation has been offered in the world of watercolor with respect to what constitutes study, that I have gone to great lengths here to present meaningful material.

Typical diagrams and analyses have been avoided, as well as various exercises that are altogether unnecessary. No advice will be given on how to paint a leaf or a tree, a clever little figure, or an industrial sky at twilight. Nor will aid be offered in the area of thatched roofs, stormy seas, stone walls, dogs, cats, horses, and birds. In my estimation, simple answers do not exist.

Nowhere in the world of art education has technique been so foolishly substituted for true meaning, self-expression, and knowledge as in the field of watercolor.

The following are examples of areas of study that are fundamental in the curricula of most top-flight art schools and colleges. It must be noted that in such a book as this, perhaps in any book, one cannot be taught *how to do*; but the following outline may well suggest *what must be done*. And while oversimplification is a deadly enemy, it is my belief that we may divide the major study areas of the painter into *composition, draftsmanship, color,* and *materials.* These four subjects are very complex in nature, and most artists become deeply involved in all at one time or another. Apropos, one may examine the work of a great painter and virtually pin-point the period when his preoccupation with one phase or another was evident. It is doubtful to me that a creative statement could be produced without the artist's being aware of all four of these subjects.

COMPOSITION

Perhaps composition, or picture structure, is the most difficult and complex of all the categories to explain, for there is little doubt that solutions to problems of composition are highly occult. By virtue of their structure alone, pictures may evoke meanings to the sensitive eye that read as legibly as realistic subject matter. Even to stand before a blank surface is to feel an intense clarity, immaculateness, and serenity. The absurdity of presenting a blank canvas for exhibition (it has been done) becomes less irrational when one contemplates the juxtaposition of emptiness next to clutter.

To digress for a moment, a painter's work may well be a daring new adventure, a reaction against other artist's efforts, past and present. His most recent paintings may take issue with his earlier work, as they strain against mannerisms, limitations, and prejudices. Composition is inexorably bound up in a reacting of one thing to another, whether or not that reaction takes place within the confines of a single painting.

Emerson once stated that "An inevitable dualism bisects nature, so that each thing is a half, and suggests another thing to make it whole; as, spirit, matter; man, woman; odd, even; subjective, objective; in, out; upper, under; motion, rest; yea, nay."

Thus, a diagonal line amidst the relative calm of perpendiculars and parallels produces activity and commotion. Large next to small, whether in color, form, mass or line, creates contrasts that are immediately felt. If a large red shape is placed next to a small green shape, we are treated simultaneously to contrasts of size and color. When two similar objects are placed side by side, one may appear to advance and the other to recede due to a simple alteration of color, tone or texture. Such investigation is so fundamental to the artist that it commences without the concerns of content and subject.

Wassily Kandinsky became so incensed with imitators (comparing them with apes) that his own approach to art remained in the area of the spiritual. A leader of the abstract movement which began in Paris at the start of the century, Kandinsky in his paintings and writings dealt not only with the basic contrasts alluded to herein, but moved on to far more esoteric areas, such as abstract "art of internal necessity."

In examining the picture plane, or surface of a painting, we find that it plays a dramatic role in how we interpret special meanings. The picture plane may invite us to look into a painting to an infinite horizon or eternity, or it may foster the illusion that objects are advancing toward us. The picture plane can support weighty architectural or geometric forms, or, conversely, the atmospheric and ethereal. Diagonal planes or planes parallel to the picture's surface may be utilized, each with different messages. The use of perspective devices, or their negation, such as the Cubist's *inversion* of perspective, is effective. We are all aware of railroad tracks appearing to converge at a distant horizon. When we upset this natural phenomenon by not allowing the tracks to converge or by widening them as they move to the horizon, we reverse order and cause the distance to advance. In essence we are dealing with distortion, a twisting or deviation from a natural shape. In further manipulating the picture plane, we use such things as surface patterns and symbols. Generally speaking, complex patterns recede as we associate smallness with distance, while the reverse is true with large patterns. Symbols such as letters of the alphabet, numbers, arrows, or other familiar shapes, also play an important role in juggling the picture plane.

The artist-composer is a keen observer of natural, architectural, and animal forms and may depend entirely upon their evolution as a source for his imagery. Or he may rely upon the imagery, subconscious, and the unpredictable (accidental). There are methods of weaving shapes to create patterns, to induce movement and produce stronger impact. Line, pattern, color, contrast, and texture support, define, and control these shapes. The very heart of a painting may reside in the fine balance of positive and negative shapes, or, to put it another way, areas that appear as weight-forms as opposed to air-spaces.

Nothing could be more appropriate today than to emphasize space, yet the artist has been dependent upon the implications and uses of space since the Stone Age. The classic use of space in Oriental and Renaissance art is illuminating, but no more so than the use of space in the contemporary works of the Surrealist, Abstract Expressionist, or Reductive painter. The control of space, whether shallow or deep, is of inestimable worth to the artist.

Lastly, a working knowledge of the traditional classic structures and controls, such as the Golden Section and/or Dynamic Symmetry, is rewarding. The Golden Section is essentially a geometrical proportion, dating back to Euclid, which governs the harmony of proportionate relationships both in art and nature. There are actually two propositions set down in Books II and VI of Euclid, but the common formula is "To cut a finite line so that the shorter part is to the longer part as the longer part is to the whole." Dynamic Symmetry is also highly geometrical. It proposes methods of establishing a series of *root rectangles* possessing perfect order comparable to that found in the Golden Section. Then, through a strict method of establishing diagonals, followed by horizontal and vertical divisions within the original shape, an endless series of lines, angles, and smaller shapes may be constructed, all in perfect proportion to one another as well as to the original shape.

One must be careful with such rigid teachings, since there is a temptation to adopt them as a crutch; but in a sense this may be said about all advice given in life. There was a time in my own career when the study of Dynamic Symmetry was an invaluable aid and comfort to me, and while my efforts at that time were self-consciously stiff and geometric, the experience was necessary.

DRAFTSMANSHIP

When one thinks of draftsmanship, perhaps the first subjects that come to mind are people, animals, and other recognizable objects. While these subjects will always be valid, there are, in addition, vast areas of expressive draftsmanship that are devoted to drawing those shapes and forms that reside only in the artist's mind. Even to play an ovoid body in tangent to a simple oblong and to do it with complete control and conviction is still draftsmanship. To carry a thrust to its wanted terminus requires not only the facility of hand, but, of far more import, the knowledge of *when* the precise goal has been reached. In painting, as with so many other things in life, the simple and direct statement can be far more difficult to achieve than the complex.

If we were to examine drawing only as drawing, that is, not as an inseparable element found in fine painting, then we might appreciate the importance that schools of art place upon good draftsmanship. For drawing is the penmanship of the artist, his very heartbeat and soul. So much is revealed in the artist's ability to draw (or his lack of it) that many great painters are truly draftsmen in color. Leonardo da Vinci, for example, was a far more exceptional draftsman than painter. It may be equally shown that a great colorist is rarely a brilliant draftsman. Bonnard and Vuillard, who without question rank among the noted colorists of our time, could hardly be classified as magnificent draftsmen.

It is vital that the painter have a working knowledge of the human form. There are countless arguments posed today, convincing enough on the surface, that take issue with this idea. We cannot deny, however, that a study of human anatomy and its function is a most revealing exposé of the ultimate in mechanical engineering. While a knowledge of all animal forms is worthwhile, and sometimes imperative, the human form remains most important for the artist.

To have a knowledge of the human form is to understand one of the most ingenious apparatuses ever designed. It would be pure folly to ignore the opportunity and need to comprehend the function of bone and muscle, or the system of joints, shock absorbers, and protective devices that make up the human anatomy. How rewarding to investigate the interior regions and become involved with the phenomena of man's physiology. Indeed, how do we understand anything until first we understand ourselves? Furthermore, how can we expect to proceed with a visual commentary involving man without clearly understanding such things? It is often stated that if you can draw the human form well, you can then draw anything well. To a large extent I believe this to be true.

There is much to be gained from the study of man's inventions and constructions. How things work together, assist or oppose one another, and hence serve as lessons in functional analysis, is of great concern. Careful exploration of architectural form, past and present, is an exciting course of study for the draftsman. The most important lesson to be gained from this area is the full appreciation of soundness in structure. The budding artist will profit from a careful inspection of machines and tools, roads and waterways, and dams and bridges, and from this study he will develop a vital awareness of force, leverage, tension, compression, and power. It is fundamentally necessary for the artist to thoroughly comprehend gravity and balance, and it is additionally rewarding for him to investigate flight, motion, and animation. He will continually draw from the vast reservoir of nature study, geography, and ultimately the new geography of other planets.

Some of his drawings may spring directly from a subconscious image, while others may ramble on to exquisite, unpredictable conclusions without apparent direction or motivation. We could not begin to account for this immense variation in detail. It is reasonable to conclude that all artists, and most especially the young so rightfully engaged in new experiences, would profit from *early* study of the foregoing outline.

When we attempt to interpret a city, a girl, or a machine through our affection or knowledge of form, depth, shape or image, tone, space, color, texture, pattern, line, mass, void, and transition, we are simply staggered by how much there is to learn. Knowledge or information comes to us in many ways, but for the artist there is nothing superior as a learning process to careful investigative drawing. The artist whose background includes such a program of study develops a deep and lasting curiosity about all that surrounds him.

COLOR

It is easy to understand that many of today's painters find color to be the most fascinating part of their work. There is so much to be known about color and its effects upon man that one can hardly limit this enormous investigation to the artist alone. It is significant too that our broad knowledge of color is relatively new. Not only does the artist continue to make startling discoveries, but men of science and medicine contribute as well.

A painter may achieve overwhelming effects through nothing more than playful experimentation with color, whereas this is not likely to occur with draftsmanship or picture structure. Therefore, color becomes a tantalizing and delicious morsel, beckoning all and seemingly within the grasp of the novice painter. One must keep in mind the admonition and gentle warning of Matisse to those who would claim to "construct by color alone" (see page 40).

For our purposes we may think of color in the area of *color physics* or *color pigment.* Most painters agree that there is a need to gain a working knowledge of both subjects, although there are those artists who carry the study of color to complex and mysterious scientific goals. Rarely do these men continue to produce creative paintings, although we find an exception to be the renowned Josef Albers.

In color physics, we are primarily concerned with colors produced by refraction, although there are other ways of generating color. The simplest demonstration of color refraction is the Newtonian experiment of directing white light through a prism, which in turn disperses the ray and produces the color spectrum. Using this as a base, the eager young artist plunges into the study of light rays and wavelengths, why objects appear to be a specific color (through the rules of color subtraction), and on into the world of psychophysiological color. For color must be a *seen* thing, requiring not only the optical but the cerebral participation of the viewer. When color experiments are conducted with such goals as the phenomena of afterimage, illusion, etc., they are usually reliant upon the comparison and contrast of color.

How chromatic or intense one color may be when played next to another, or how dark or light a tone, or how warm or cool one color may appear through various juxtapositions offer endless and exciting challenges to the serious art student. A former teacher of mine, a noted color authority, has successfully identified color while blindfolded by placing his fingertips over multi-hued surfaces exposed to heat. Since it is basic knowledge that black absorbs and white refracts heat, it would not be too difficult for anyone to succeed with a very simple experiment of his own.

The painter and his pigment, in contrast to the color scientist, works in many other areas. He begins with a very basic use of color spirituality; in other words, he uses color to evoke emotional conditions within the viewer. For example, we all react to blues and greens, or the *cooler* spectrum, quite differently from reds and oranges, or the *warmer* spectrum. Color combinations may easily provide for us any number of harmonious or dissonant reactions. Color symbology, elaborated upon below, is especially significant to the artist in attaining more esoteric, precise meanings. Color impressionism is undoubtedly the most widely accepted area (although not easily understood) to be explored by the artist; this is largely due to the popularity of the Impressionist painters. Color groupings that provide the viewer with sensations of humidity and temperature, as suggested by the terms *warmer* and *cooler* noted above, prove to be invaluable to the painter. Lastly, artists will explore the areas of precise color construction, which are often extremely mathematical. Apropos, there are methods and theories to be dissected. The Munsell system presents strict measurements for all color with respect to hue, value, and chroma. The Ostwald color system classifies all colors as either achromatic or chromatic, with a peculiar and complicated method of descriptions such as *full-clear colors*, *light-clear colors*, and *tones*. The great men of color are to be sought out; in particular Goethe, Bezold, Chevreul (who influenced the Impressionists), Holzel, Itten, and Albers.

When we think of the symbolic meanings of color, we automatically visualize red and green as stop and go. Red, white, and blue may hold deep implication for the American or the Englishman, but what kind of meaning does it hold for the Mexican? In America the color black is a funereal symbol, while in China it is white. Religion is filled with color symbolism: specific colors are associated with various rites and feasts. We need look no further than the red and green of Christmas and the blue and white of Hanukkah. White was once believed to be hygienically advantageous and was considered necessary in hospitals, especially operating rooms. Yet we now know that white contributes to eye fatigue, due to the intensity of light refraction of a white surface.

So, whether we are deeply or superficially involved with color, we recognize that the chemist, the physicist, the physiologist, and the psychologist contribute constantly to our growing store of color information. And while the artist has explored in the past, and will continue to explore and discover, he, along with the architect, designer, city planner and others interested in color from every esthetic attitude, will depend upon such sources for new information.

MATERIALS

The last broad category that must concern every artist at one time or another deals with materials and equipment. Since in Sections 4 and 6 the dynamics of watercolor and related media are fully covered, and there is a section in the Appendix entitled Materials and Equipment, this account will be brief.

The artist has to be aware of his materials, the nature of his pigment, of ground and support, adhering factors, permanency, and use. He must be cognizant of known limitations of media in order to be prepared to move on to new achievements. He cannot carry out experimentation successfully without a thorough understanding of his tools and materials, nor can he reconstruct desired qualities that are gained through accident alone. He will benefit in other ways that will save him both time and expense, for there are high roads and low roads to all destinations. Apropos, to see an artist use a large brush for a minute notation, or dry paint on a porous surface, or apply sensitive tonal nuances to a buckled or warped support, or simply paint *lean over fat* seems incredible to me, especially when he does not do so through selection, for special effect.

Still we must remember that artists are not chemists or scientists, and that there is a decided limit to the emphasis placed upon technological attitudes or theories. In the long analysis, as stated elsewhere, there is only expression. Only in rare instances would the esthetic viewpoint fail to suffuse and dominate the work.

While we cannot prescribe exactly what should constitute an artist's back-

Figure with Bandaged Legs by Rico Lebrun (1900-1964). 1959. Ink wash and wax. 30 x 15¾ inches.

The power of the draftsman — what revelation, what singular beauty! The work of Lebrun needs no accolade, for it speaks its own mind. One has only to glance at *Figure with Bandaged Legs* to be swept into the world of mass and weight and of chiaroscuro and counterpoise. What a propitious moment to dwell upon the dividends of drawing knowledge. And what good fortune that the artist uses wash and line to record the moment. But here, from the magnificent volume *Rico Lebrun, Drawings* (University of California Press), the artist speaks for himself:

I shun drawing which is too easily formulated. It does not seem fertilized enough to produce consequences, and a drawing should be a provoker of consequences. It should be, above all, not a thing of art but a tool for understanding. I wish my drawing to get richer by consulting the tangible world. I am just beginning to see how even the most static form is bounded by profiles so constantly changing that the form itself is in movement. This inherent animation which has nothing to do with action offers me a chance to select and transfer to the paper those contours which most fully describe that movement and that life. When I become arbitrary in my selection, the drawing weakens; it is at this point that elegance, spontaneity, and freshness often take over and essentially destroy meaning.

The fine edge between the pertinent and the brilliant can be maintained only with the greatest effort. On the other hand, the deceptively simple means of line can lead time and again to half-truths. Seemingly the most easy of all crafts, drawing is the one which reveals most tellingly our incapacity to sustain true vision and our acquiescence to the ready-made. This baffling fact has haunted the work of even some of the greatest master draftsmen. And the nature of the task has all along been so strenuous that it is easy to see why drawing in our own time has moved violently away from the contest with the ascertainable world. Not only did it not want to repeat the results of the masters of the past (a moral resolution to be fully endorsed), but it could not find symbols of its own potent enough to equal in validity what tradition had already achieved. And in trying to find a new world of its own, the line — living into itself, disengaging itself more and more — finally achieved an ironical independence which is fine to see but not nourishing to the soul.

ground of study, it would be well if he could look back upon such exposure as is outlined above. Even then it is doubtful if anything more than a small progress would have been made in any direction. The true artist never really terminates the study program, for he is constantly searching and uncovering. This is part of his nature. Picasso states that he does not search any longer, but instead discovers, and this may very well be valid. Artists may play with semantics a bit, especially when paraphrasing Picasso; but all great artists learn and grow until stripped of the ability to work.

Whether an artist *searches* or *discovers* seems irrelevant to me at this point. What is important is that through intensive and thorough training, the young or beginning artist is led toward that golden moment when he will feel released from all bonds and fully prepared to begin. What precise order his training takes is continually debated by artists and educators, since needs vary with the individual student. Training, whether gained in formal institutions or otherwise, breeds discipline, and all great artists possessed some form of discipline. How else might one discard or violate rules, unless they have been learned; for to deny or *non-conform*, one must be intimate with the facts of one's rebellion, and anything less is deceptive or juvenile.

Sleeping Women (page from Shelter Sketchbook), by Henry Moore (b. 1898). 1941. Watercolor, ink, and gouache.

Undoubtedly the most renowned sculptor of the 20th century, Henry Moore is noted for his poignant draftsmanship, particularly his epic drawings of sleepers in the underground shelters of London during the Second World War. The name and work of Moore will invariably be included in any discussion of art today, but why, you may ask, is it deemed particularly necessary in a book which is devoted primarily to watercolor? The answer is extremely simple: Henry Moore employs watercolor in its purest and noblest form; that is to say, one is hardly aware of its presence. Its place has been subordinated to a supporting role, with the result that all emphasis is given to meaning.

We turn to Moore for yet another reason: his is a unique force and direction that broadens the horizon of watercolor. He does not overwhelm or shout as does the magnificent Lebrun on the opposite page; but instead he gnaws at your soul and conscience. The work shown here is typical of that distinctive power, as it plays upon us with an incisive and tender message. One runs the emotional gamut, sensing courage and fatigue, and feeling guilt or shame. The attack is persistent; there is no relief. The artist's compassion is overwhelming.

Henry Moore was born at Castleford, England, of a family of miners. Today he works in an ancient farmhouse near Hertfordshire, a rural community just north of London. The monumentality of his sculpture is known to all, but an equally impressive attribute of Moore is his personal integrity and character. This always seemed so to me in his interviews and writings; it was also quite evident in our brief correspondence.

While of secondary importance, it should be noted that the trying conditions under which Mr. Moore worked during the brutal bombing of London compelled him to rely upon the special advantages of watercolor.

Group of Three Girls by Egon Schiele (1890-1918). 1911. Pencil and watercolor. 12¼ x 17¾ inches.

Nowhere can there be found a more significant contribution to the world of watercolor than the work of Egon Schiele. And yet the wedding of medium and artist is far removed from the mastery of Lebrun or the calm of Henry Moore. Instead, we are confronted with torture and struggle, along with constant argument and futility. No less compassionate than the others, and unquestionably a brilliant draftsman, Schiele stood apart as a young genius on the prowl, searching and demanding as he went.

Egon Schiele died in 1918 at the tender age of 28, thus terminating a most promising career (see page 35). A dedicated student of Gustav Klimt, he was well on his way toward the development of a highly inquisitive, peculiar approach without precedent. While *Group of Three Girls* is relatively serene, there remains an underlying feeling of deep concern for the girls, perhaps even of impending tragedy. This characteristic is not foreign to Schiele's work, whether it is still life, landscape or the figure. While Schiele did some work in oil, most of his efforts were executed in watercolor and, to great extent, concerned themselves with portraiture or attitudes of the human body.

The intriguing analogy to be found here is that the manner in which Schiele abuses the medium fits neatly into the content-message he offers. One is compelled to accept the fact that this is not purely accidental, indeed it remains at the very core of his work; but there is a lingering impression that this was also the way it had to be, that there was no choice. He was an intense young man who had little use for convention. His work sought out the truth as he saw it, concealed nothing, and avoided the accepted genre of the day.

Over and over again we are made aware of the union of drawing knowledge and personal concept. One could hardly point to a mastery of the medium in the conventional sense, or begin to instruct in Schiele's style; it would prove fruitless. Egon Schiele not only assaults accepted notions of how one ought to draw, but utterly ignores all technical painting advice as well.

COURTESY OF THE VIENNA ALBERTINA.

The City (Man and Woman) by George Grosz (1893-1959). 1930-31. Watercolor. 25½ x 18½ inches.

We have examined the work of three brilliant draftsmen working with watercolor, Rico Lebrun, Henry Moore, and Egon Schiele. The fourth, George Grosz, though equally competent, is unique. The Grosz legacy is filled with an unparalleled bitterness. The nature of his enemies demanded savage reaction, and George Grosz met the challenge head-on. He lashed out at war profiteers, their promoters, and the establishment with a hatred that was born of deep belief. He dealt with sexual perversion, greed, lust, and crime with an eye to awakening the working class to all that was around them. He was utterly fearless and spared no one. Hitler and Nazi Germany ultimately became one of his chief targets; it finally became necessary for him to flee his country and seek refuge in the United States.

The satirical genius of Grosz has been so well established that few are aware of his other qualities as a painter. Subject matter or message alone does not automatically will greatness to a work of art, nor does the mere facility scorned by Nicolaides. The fact that the thoroughly trained Grosz saw and felt an enormous human injustice truly allowed him wider latitude and gives our thesis deeper meaning.

This relatively passive example of his work begins with the enigmatic double title, *The City (Man and Woman)*. It is as if Grosz wanted much more to be perceived than just an affluent couple out for a stroll. Their fashionable attire, and the suggestion of a wintry night in the lighted city, summon subjective responses, as does the brisk action of the massive man pulling along with giant strides his more delicate companion.

As *The City* attests, Grosz is at ease with subject and media. He controls fluid wash and line with less concern for method than for his esthetic goal. In his widely known *Ecce Homo* series, he is far more caustic and violent in his attack upon a depraved society but, oddly, not as spontaneous as in *The City*. Whatever his direction, Grosz was a brilliant draftsman whose limitations knew no boundaries.

No artist may be adjudged by a single work; in Grosz's case such an attempt would be pure folly. Throughout his turbulent life, his work reflected one eventful turning after another. Court-martialed and saved from the death penalty, fined again and again for "insulting" works aimed at the army and public morality, he nevertheless continued to produce throughout his life. Although he became an American citizen, George Grosz was ultimately accepted and honored by his native Germany.

COLLECTION OF THE LOS ANGELES COUNTY MUSEUM.

Flowers Cyclamen by Charles Demuth (1883-1935). 1920. Watercolor on paper. 11¾ x 13¾ inches.

Whatever Demuth painted was done with extreme care, as is evident in this meticulous study of flowers. Whether working from vaudeville entertainers, flowers, or factories, his patient attitude robbed nothing from the effectiveness of his paintings.

Charles Demuth was an excellent draftsman and an even more remarkable composer. His illustrations of the works of Poe, Zola, and Henry James rank high as collector's items, while his paintings of acrobats are sought after by museum curators everywhere. But the relatively serene painting of cyclamens reveals more for our purposes than do his other works. Here Demuth exposes a penchant for control which faintly echoes the Cubist manner,

an influence he openly admitted and which was even more evident in his paintings of architecture. Demuth's control of space and form, along with his ability to transpose dark and light, invests his paintings with imminent drama bordering on the sinister. While it may seem far-fetched to those who are not aware of Charles Demuth's full range, he was considered to be a modernist crusader and is now acknowledged to be a forerunner of Pop art.

A by John Altoon (1925-1969). 1956. Gouache on board. 29¾ by 40 inches.

There are no rules, nor is there need for any, to explain this exquisite work by John Altoon. Here we find the same considerations of surface and plane, dark and light, and form and space that appear in the preceding paintings in this book. However, there is no trace of subject, apart from insinuations, and the painting continually serves as a springboard for the individual imagination and occult appetite.

Always a brilliant craftsman, Altoon offers an intriguing tactile experience in his painting. Enormous, monolithic masses seem to float weightlessly in space, suggesting form through essentially flattened shapes. The painting is not a depiction of some object or person, but the beginning of a new and private point of departure for each viewer.

River at the Bridge of Trois Sautets by Paul Cézanne (1839-1906). 1906. Watercolor on paper.

On Morse Mountain, Small Point, Maine by John Marin (1870-1953). 1928. Watercolor. 21 x 16½ inches.

How frustrating only to mention Cézanne and Marin. To expect single paintings to represent their massive contributions to art is unthinkable. Their contributions cannot be summed up by their works alone, but must be reflected against their roles as leaders of great art movements in Europe and America.

Since so much has been written about these two painters, we need not delve too deeply into folklore, but instead come directly to the point. We are examining their work with a single thought in mind: to uncover evidence of master composers at work.

It is by careful intent that we pose Cézanne's tranquility against the blast of Marin; yet one painting complements the other, and neither suffers by comparison because each artist remains in full control of total orchestration. Cézanne thought *River at the Bridge of Trois Sautets* to be one of his most harmonious efforts, achieving the utmost possible relationships. Every element in this sensitively structured painting seems indispensable. The rhythms, movements, films of iridescent color, and soft staccato line summon forth a vibrant melody. There is supreme order and ceaseless enjoyment to be found in repeated viewing. It is a magic blending of invitation and distant recollection, unquestionably the stamp of Cézanne. Painted during the last summer of his life, it survives as a dividend of his enormous dedication.

At first glance, *On Morse Mountain* seems quite different from Cézanne's painting; yet, when carefully analyzed, it is quite similar. Despite his more rugged approach, John Marin was as deeply concerned as Cézanne with the total statement and picture plane. Marin was a crusty, outdoor soul who abhorred convention, and his work reflected this character. Imbued with a love of nature, he was dedicated to a perception built upon a full use of the senses. He leaned into the wind and filled his lungs with the salt air; he meant his work to lure the viewer into this world. His enthusiasm caused him to paint over margins and onto the frame, at the same time dividing, cutting, and creating new planes within the painting's surface wherever needed.

In both of these notable statements concerning nature, there is no need for more horizon. Each painter says what he must and is done, and neither work pretends to be more through embellishment or geographical identification. Cézanne gives us a tender word, a quatrain; Marin grabs and sweeps us out to sea; but the compositional genius of both artists is omnipresent.

COLLECTION OF MR. H. SAGE GOODWIN. PHOTO PETER A. JULEY & SON.

Untitled by Sam Francis (b. 1923). 1953. Watercolor on paper. 20¼ x 25⅝ inches.

Our color essay begins with this glowing statement by Sam Francis and will include the work of Jean Dubuffet, Ernst Wilhelm Nay, and Keith Crown. Each of these painters has placed so much emphasis upon color that it would be meaningless to view his work in black and white.

Sam Francis has long been recognized as one of the most dramatic of contemporary colorists. As revealed on this page, his work rings with an exceptional chromatic vibrancy. His brush darts furiously over the surface, combines with splatters and drippings, and builds toward a thun-derous crescendo. His control is so complete that the experience is re-lived with each viewing.

While Francis exploits the full color spectrum, it is rewarding to note how carefully he distributes his hues. At first glance, the viewer is aware of a large, essentially cool, blue mass moving against a red-orange space. Yet within the warmer and lighter spatial areas are countless minute, cool accents which activate and provide fuller meaning. Sunken into the major blue mass are the most exquisite nuances of warm and cool greens, pinks, violets, and rich ultramarine blues, again completing the warm-cool balance so desirable in gaining color temperature.

54

Jardin Nacre by Jean Dubuffet (b. 1901). 1955. Collage with butterfly wings and watercolor. 8⅜ x 11⅝ inches.

Jean Dubuffet is represented here by an exquisite example of his work in watercolor with butterfly wings. When his friend Pierre Bettencourt developed this approach, Dubuffet openly expressed his fascination with the method and produced many small paintings.

One may question why *Jardin Nacre* should be part of a color essay, for surely it is not overpowering in either content or color. But for this reason alone, it is a commendable foil to play against the Sam Francis opposite. Dubuffet's singular goal is bound up with the premise of a delicate, restrained, dominating light-warm color; yet we note that he feels compelled carefully to fit a few small, cool grays and blues into his scheme. *Jardin Nacre* (or, translated, *Pearly Garden*) recreates for the viewer the same magnetic powers that initially enthralled Dubuffet.

Composition by Ernst Wilhelm Nay (b. 1902). 1965. Watercolor.

Color and the paintings of Nay are inseparable, as is evidenced by his resplendent *Composition*. One could reach blindfolded into his portfolio and extract one glorious color essay after another.

Ernst Wilhelm Nay is a colorist, color-scientist, innovator, and experimentalist. His color theories are often so complex that rarely are they meaningful to more than a handful of artists and scholars. In *Composition* we are entranced by the shifting succession of color forms, some dwindling, others rushing toward us, framed on both sides by cadent, vertical borders. Nay's subject is color, his love is color, and his paintings leave little doubt of this.

Sea and White Lines by Keith Crown (b. 1918). 1964. Watercolor. 30 by 22 inches.

Vibrancy of color has long been a trademark of Keith Crown; this dynamic statement is no exception. The towering, listing story of *Sea and White Lines* would prove effective if told in black and white alone, but Crown enlists color with great purpose. Held to relatively passive and essentially cool color nuances in the lower areas, our attention is drawn upward with increased acceleration, to erupt ultimately into a world of mighty reds, oranges, and smaller bright complements. As Crown himself has so ably written, "Everything is color. The slightest nuance has another precise meaning. Color is a language of the poet. Anything can be any color at any time depending on what color everything else is at the time."

57

THE CONTEMPORARY

Dragonade by Mark Tobey (b. 1890).
1957. Sumi ink and rice paper. 24⅝ x
34⅛ inches.

SCHOOL

Defining precisely who or what is the "contemporary school" is so difficult and subjective a task that it might very well prove an impossibility. Nothing of this nature will be attempted here, save to chronicle in part some of the work that is being executed with watercolor today. Perhaps it should be further noted that while we are fully aware of much of the art of the day, we are certainly in no way able to account for all of it. Since most artists and critics agree that *art is a very secret thing* (created by one person, usually working alone, and not always able or willing to describe his work), there is a gnawing possibility that even the galleries and museums do not contain examples of the most significant contemporary paintings. As we all know, this condition is not peculiar to the present era alone. While we know that many contemporary painters of note have been duly recognized, and their works may be seen continually in galleries, museums, or reproduced in periodicals and books, we must also surmise that there will be numerous others appearing later who will take their rightful places as important members of our contemporary school. And we can only conjecture when we attempt to appraise any of today's work in the light of its meaningful endurance.

There was a time when it seemed painfully clear that watercolor painters produced more trivia than any other group of artists. In America and England, in particular, this condition existed, for painting in watercolor was a pastime or hobby, and was even taught as such in stylish girls' schools. Or it was nothing more than a sketching device, and the results, although stimulating, were dismissed as incomplete works. Clubs, groups, or societies were formed and unwittingly fostered one approach or another, usually with a local hero and his sycophants leading the way. But even as these dilettantish adventures were taking place (and they still are in many places), solid painting in watercolor was also being produced. In America, for example, if Homer was largely responsible for elevating watercolor to a major role, then we must assume that Prendergast kept it there, and Marin gave it liberation.

In the first section we traced briefly the origin and development of painting, with special attention to the important role played by watercolor. Throughout, painting has served the purposes of documentation and decoration. There were very few deviations from the accepted premise that a painting must communicate readily to the viewer, and that subject matter should of necessity consist of recognizable objects. This was true even with Bosch's *Garden of Worldly Delights* (a precursor of surrealism), in which a most unlikely fantasy unfolds, employing carefully realized human and animal forms.

However, in the contemporary world of painting there are no such boundaries with which to contend. Over and over again we face difficulty in determining whether a painting is an oil, acrylic, or casein; or if it has been executed with transparent washes of turpentine or water bases, on canvas or paper. And this is as it should be, for the choice of medium is arrived at by a number of factors that have very little to do with predetermined limitations or restrictions.

It does not seem strange to me to note that Paul Cézanne, working in both watercolor and oil, began the great movement away from Renaissance thinking. Most scholars agree that Cézanne, at the head of the Post-Impressionist Movement, founded the modern school. There were others, too, such as Monet with his preoccupation with light, color, and their effects; but his was an unordered contribution that truly achieved full realization only with the lily-pond paintings near the end of his life. And while it was not Cézanne's desire to form a school or develop disciples (for he believed in an "individual intuition, fundamental, free from all preconceived academic ideas"), his followers were legion.

Cézanne's preoccupation with order through "concentric focusing" was not adhered to by Seurat, Pissarro, or the Pointillists. Men such as Bonnard and Vuillard seized upon a theme of dazzling quiltworks of color, while Van Gogh's concern was dynamic energy, and Gauguin's a pattern-tapestry of highly personal color. Others, such as Rouault, Picabia, Delaunay, and Leger strayed even further; yet in their work one could easily identify Cézanne's influence.

Now that Impressionism was a reality, it had to follow that there would be a continuing chain of rebellious reaction. So it was that the Fauves, or wild beasts, with Matisse as their leader, rose up to denounce Impressionism in general, and Seurat's mechanical approach in particular. In attacking "Divisionism," Matisse claimed that "The splitting of color brought the splitting up of form and contour."

Meanwhile, from Germany came Expressionism, with the two groups Die Brücke and Der Blaue Reiter spearheading the movement. Modersohn-Becker, Mueller, Pechstein, and later Nolde, Munch and Ensor, among others, were leading artists in this movement. Here was a vital, restless, and frenzied art that may well reflect the introspective, self-examining, and sometimes morbid temperament of the northern European mind. A sense of fear, imminence, fantasy, and mystery are inescapable throughout the Expressionists' work. In addition, we continually see Gauguin's strong influence; he, in turn, was greatly motivated by the printmakers of Japan. But if such imbrication in those days seems startling to some, think how prevalent it is today with supersonic travel and instant communication at our disposal. "Schools," as we have so conveniently labeled them in the past, no longer reflect provincial points of view but are now of necessity international in style.

To return to the events leading up to the present school of painting, it remained for the Cubists to create the most remarkable turn of all. Not only did their art influence the world of painting then and now, but it spilled over into architecture and design as well. The grandeur and elegance of Cubist paintings, at first colorless, fragmented and geometrically shaped, remains to this day. Later, as the work became more colorful and prismatic, it developed such a

60

dominantly scientific nature that it was likened to the work of Seurat. While it is sometimes impossible to pin-point a precise origin, it is generally conceded that two of contemporary art's strongest tendencies sprang from the work of the Cubists. One is the lesson of simultaneity, in which, as an example, one sees the interior of a vessel as well as its profile at the same time. The other is inverted perspective, in which lines, instead of converging as they move away from the viewer, grow farther apart. One may witness these devices at work throughout Cubist work, and most especially in the paintings of Juan Gris.

Futurism, while not of Cubist import, nonetheless contributed immensely to the artist's development of motion symbols: time and speed. Undoubtedly everyone concerned with art knows of the outrageous reaction to Duchamp's *Nude Descending a Staircase.* After its appearance at the Armory Exhibition in New York in 1913, Duchamp and *Nude* were household words in America. Less well known is the manifesto of the Futurists, speaking out against virtually everything and anything, including imitation, the masters, harmony, and good taste.

There is little doubt that the Dadaists had the most profound and lasting effect upon the trends that are current in our time. While the hub of this movement lay in Europe, as did all of the other schools noted herein, Dada quickly took on an international flavor. Major cities in Germany, Italy, Spain, Switzerland, and France formed Dada groups, and proceeded to hold festivals and fairs, to publish and exhibit. In New York, Alfred Stieglitz and his gallery became the center of the modern movement, displaying works of both European and American artists. It is of special interest to us that John Marin was a charter member of the Stieglitz stable, for this pioneer of the American moderns worked almost exclusively in watercolor.

Dadaism was in essence a denouncement of naturalism, realism, and idealism; in other words, imitation of nature was a lie! It dealt a death blow to those who were tenaciously guarding traditional ideas, and at the same time created a wedge into the future. And the Dada Movement was not to be confined to painting alone. It was a source of inspiration for poets, writers, and architects of the era. It became a symbol of freedom to men such as Schwitters, whose work made out of junk and rubbish was intended to shock the bourgeoisie. It is not surprising to find an even stronger bond between the Dada artists and those of today, when one realizes that there is a continuing protest against a society that embraces warfare. And because of a deepened sense of outrage and disgust, it is understandable, if not reasonable, that much of today's art is absurd, self-devouring, or *anti-art.*

Surrealism, the last movement of note that we shall concern ourselves with in this brief résumé, was soon to follow the Dadaists. But it is debatable if the Surrealists did more than bring attention to an art form that may well enjoy immortality. The ubiquitous nature of an artist's intimate fantasy world is made of such revealing stuff that it could never be denied. This is not to say that the Surrealist vision is universally accepted as the epitome of expression; incongruously, it is viewed with disgust by hordes of artists. The major source of resentment might well be the tedious use of photo-reality, despite the bizarre or dreamlike content couched in pronounced psychological overtones. But my point is, at the risk of oversimplification, that we have noted the works of Bosch, Arcimboldo, and Jamnitzer from as far back as the 15th Century, which appear as contemporary as many modern Surrealist attempts. Dali, who is considered by some to be the leading exponent of Surrealist thinking (this view is not shared by all artists or critics), has virtually repeated examples of both Arcimboldo and Larmessin. The contributions of Ernst, Arp, Masson, Miró, Magritte, and Tanguy, among others, live on as far more distinguished Surrealist works.

While there have been numerous other influences felt since the advent of Surrealism, it does not appear that any clearly defined "school" of great import has been established. Nor does it suit our purposes to even presume evaluation or identification of such recent art. We cannot neglect reference to Action Painting and its marriage to emotion, vitality, and intoxicating drives. In this area alone, Jackson Pollock led the way toward international recognition of the contemporary American painter. And while Pollock was not the sole originator of action painting as such, he was immensely successful and well accepted at the time of his unfortunate death, and left a scintillating bequest to the contemporary world of art.

Today there are newer and newer turnings. Pop and Op art have been on the scene for some time. At the moment, there are eventful things being done in the realm of Psychedelic and Reductive art, both with paint and light. Happenings, boxes, traps, found objects, assemblage, frottage, and numerous other names, descriptions, and manifestos inundate us. Some directions are real, meaningful, and durable, if not much more than a repetition or extension of the earlier movements chronicled here.

To resume our discussion of the contemporary school, or (a) that part of it working in watercolor, and (b) artists who work in watercolor now and then, let me make the following clear. There is convincing proof that the versatility of watercolor is well established. Additionally, there is a long record of artists from every school and era who have felt compelled to employ watercolor for one reason or another. But nowhere is there to be found any work of lasting import that is referred to by medium over content. If it be said "the etchings of Rembrandt" or "the watercolors of Turner," it most assuredly is not the method or technique that is uppermost in mind (save perhaps for pedantic discussion), but rather the content-meaning of great artistic accomplishment.

Nor can watercolor be dismissed to a minor role, for quantity will never equal quality. It is enervating to read essays and theories espousing naive reasons for watercolor ever to have existed. The last such diagnosis to come my way binds American watercolor securely to "luminism," as if this were the major goal of Marin, Burchfield, Tobey, O'Keeffe, or Francis, to name but a few American artists of stature whose work in watercolor is well known to us.

The following pages devoted to paintings by artists working in watercolor is by no means a complete register of all such contemporary work of note. It is work that is either known to me by my association with the artist, knowledge of his work, and/or its availability for this purpose. Furthermore, I feel compelled to offer my deepest apologies to the numerous artists whose work would merit inclusion, but, by the very nature of physical limitations, has been omitted. Since the paintings have been selected to present as comprehensive a viewpoint as possible, without attempting a complete bibliography, each artist has been asked to present a written statement concerning his attitudes, concerns, and beliefs. In this way we may gain further insight into the unique autobiographical nature of watercolor and its content.

Pipe Dream by Edward Reep. 1967. Watercolor and ink on rice paper. 8½ x 12 inches.

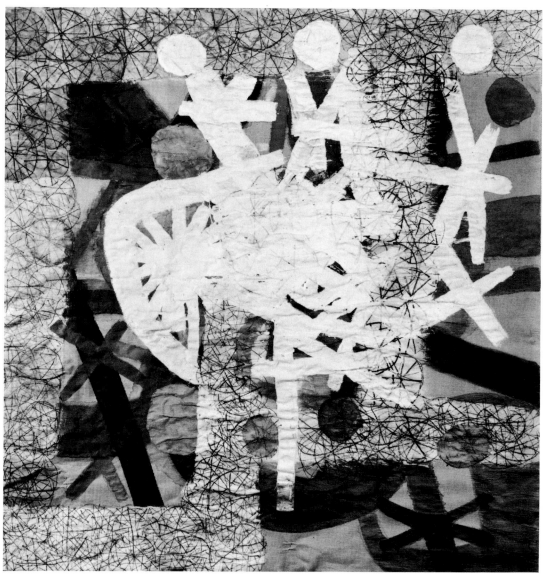

Fugue in the Silence #15 by Hilda Levy. 1963. Watercolor on "hospital paper." 19½ x 19½ inches.

In talking about painting, words may become a trap! The trap springs from man's need for reference to the known, the familiar — a sense of security. In seeking to hold on to these bases, one may fail to keep his emotional and mental passages open for the unfamiliar. The finality of the word is a deadening thing!

The visual arts offer the possibility to keep open these channels for true experience through revelation. This involves a process of becoming. The process of continuous change, or metamorphosis, is truly man's link with the Universe. This vision being metamorphic, how can the artist define his art? The nature of the creative self is so illusive, unknowable! The truth of the now stands by the side of a further revealment of the tomorrow.

A painting is telling of a creative act or of a non-creative act.

The process of life experience moves toward extraction of essences. Extraction follows destruction of elements made unnecessary for the moment present. So, too, in the painting — the process of destruction moves to preserve the necessary only.

The painting presents in itself the full gamut of an all-inclusive experience, and through its metamorphic existence continues to a composite of essentials. This final abstraction brings forth a new truth.

An attempt at explanation of a painting begins its dissolution. It will, however, reveal of its own accord its mystery to the beholder patiently seeking to fathom its meaning.

The fulfillment of the painting is the sensing of its particular flow as a truth. Only this experience can give the work a life of its own.

(Hilda Levy)

64

Three P.M. Fog by N. P. Brigante (b. 1895). 1962. Watercolor and ink on paper. 24 x 36 inches.

The artist must have absolute control from start to completion over all forces that engender the creative effort. This includes control over craftsmanship and materials, the entire surface and the spaces confronting him, the elements which suggest movement and dynamic, kinetic energy (Yang, active, male), and those which promote tranquility, with the rest and repose that follow (Yin, passive, female).

The artist synchronizes ends and means as well as heart and brain.

The natural world remains as always the common basis for all inspiration and research, even though it has changed from the world of our fathers and of antiquity. New images are constantly discovered and revealed, and appear in ever-changing forms for both our pleasure and enjoyment. We are also inundated with new sights, sounds, tastes, textures, and smells. To understand this new development, we must re-make and re-orient our vision with these new images, in order to direct these new elements into concrete, permanent, and expressive art forms. They possess shapes and are confined within limits, and they are microscopically small as well as enormous . . . Furthermore, these many images may reveal themselves to us but for a fleeting moment.

This nature touches and immerses us in a moving sea of atmosphere, heat, dampness, and cold. We are awed by the mystery contained within the volume of its depth and space.

(From *The Artist's Approach to the New Nature* by Nick Brigante.)

Composition by Ernst Wilhelm Nay (b. 1902). 1964. Watercolor. 16½ x 23¾ inches.

The notable simplicity of Nay's spontaneous and melodious paintings, would at first seem to contradict his elaborate philosophical premises. But quite the opposite is true, for he is totally reliant upon his personal investigations as source material for his efforts.

Nay is imbued with "the loneliness of man," and alludes to this in his writings. Initially I considered translating his statements verbatim, but all of my efforts proved meaningless. As his erudite wife Elisabeth has written to me (in English), ". . . But Nay's language is the language of an artist, and is sometimes not logical."

It is logical enough for us to determine that there is a brilliant and sensitive mind at work when Nay paints. "Nature," he states, "is not only visual, but has mathematical form." He draws from nature experiences which allow his work to speak of these experiences rather than of nature itself. He speaks of time, space, mathematics, physics, and cosmology as prime sources for new thoughts. He writes with abstract precision of ascending and diminishing scales of color and movement motifs. His treatises include the analysis of the number as a symbol, posing value against its imminent value.

Nay's paintings project an eternal quality that extends beyond the borders of the frame. He feels that his work is non-visual at first viewing, but that it becomes more and more visual as we reach the center of each painting, where the visual quality disappears again. He likens this phenomenon to "a wave flowing over the painting in a very poetic way." This continual movement in each painting establishes the basis for a genesis; that is, the energy of one work flows into or demands another, until an ultimate cycle is completed. In his numerous exhibitions, Nay very positively wants each painting to be in contact with the next, in order to form this *zyklus,* or cycle.

Untitled by Watson Cross (b. 1918). 1965. Casein watercolor. 19 x 28 inches.

As an artist-teacher I find many direct parallels in my approach to art and to my classes. There must be an opening of oneself, a freeing of one's tensions, prejudices, and predetermined techniques, to make contact, whether it be with a canvas or a student. Contact is the precise word. One must strip away one's surface self or front, one's respectability, in a sense, and say, "This is me! Take me, or reject me, but by God, this is me! This is my painting, this is my line!"

This sounds egotistical. What presumption to say, "I'm an artist," and, even more, "I'm a teacher of art." The brief history of watercolor painting included in this book can make one feel mighty humble. What a colossal act of egotism, then, to paint yet another picture! This is a part of the "hang-up" that must be stripped away if we are to make contact anew, to again be Adam before the Fall, or the child-artist before school.

As existential as the above may sound, we need not separate ourselves from the world of everyday experiences. In fact, these very experiences can enrich and mature us if we give ourselves to them.

Contact with new materials as well as with vital new people can bring creative action and touch new facets of the inner self. Knowing these inner resources and not undervaluing them in the slightest, we should prepare our physical self with the skills, crafts, and mechanics that seem continuingly relevant to our field. If we are unprepared technically, this too can limit our freedom and creativity.

When your precious moment of contact comes, prepared or not, it's your picture, or thing, happening then and for the first time.

(Watson Cross)

Dream by Leonard Edmondson (b. 1916). 1964. Watercolor collage. 19½ x 28½ inches.

Each artist creates out of an environment. His environment is physical, emotional, and intellectual — and he is imprisoned by it. What the artist receives (perceives) and how he responds (re-creates) are two faces which peer over his shoulder as he works. He may glorify his environment or curse it, embrace it or flee from it, make it a tomb or make it a garden, but he cannot turn away from the reality of it. This environment is made up of the major philosophical and social trends of his day on the one hand, and the most trivial, fragmentary, and peripheral episodes on the other.

The environment in which I work is dominated by science and technology. The machine has taken over and is my teacher. Science has created the specters of over-population and annihilation. An industrialized urban society has destroyed the old myths, scattered the family, and alienated man from nature, from his work, and from his fellow man. In the face of this environment that is shaping my art, I have responded in two ways. My first response is to assume an anti-traditional attitude — one that turns away from the familiar, the ingratiating, the appealing; one that defies limitations of artistic vocabulary (concepts, attitudes, purposes). My second response is to identify with the existentialists' "absurd man," who prefers to live with his courage and his reasoning, to live without appeal within the span of his lifetime — the artist who does not concern himself with creating for posterity, but only with those creative acts which fulfill his existence.

My creative acts are intellectually conceived and pursued, with little reliance on gesture and still less on informality. The technique is impersonal (not the handwriting of the artist). The painting solutions are based on a predetermined structure (primarily of space, but also of arrangement). Space is sometimes used like an atmosphere which surrounds shapes and objects; sometimes like a web on which shapes cling. The arrangements can become either active (swift, moving, dynamic) or static (slow-moving or even inanimate). I would like my work to engage the viewer, to provoke him, to leave him free. My work is not didactic. It does not teach; it shares. It is its own metaphor. Its roots are buried in the environment from which it springs.

(Leonard Edmondson)

Oracle by Leonard Cutrow (b. 1911). 1962. Watercolor and ink on cloth. 14½ x 15½ inches.

It is difficult to write about one's own painting, since it must speak for itself; therefore, I will comment on painting in general. By painting I mean the artist's constant search for new symbols and ways to communicate.

The artist, from long, striving study, becomes keenly attuned to form; attuned to so great a degree that on rare occasions he develops new symbols and new ways of using this broad language. He applies these symbols in his own particular way of seeing and executing; he manipulates his vast energies to make use of all directions and accidents. He pushes and seeks because of a momentary mood. He gam-bles and sometimes succeeds, then judges the work and in retrospect justifies the logic — a logic that does not necessarily come from the status quo.

Therefore, the artist with all of his concepts encompasses a broad range of human acts in the creation of a work of art.

(Leonard Cutrow)

Malibu Series by Jack Kling (b. 1929). 1967. Ink on rice paper. 20 x 30 inches.

Ink drop falls, splashes, spreads; another follows, and another, and still more. From somewhere a line appears; it is intersected by another, and soon, as if by magic, shapes take form and meaning.

In a few seconds the intensity of feeling dissipates and is lost forever.

I try again and again, finding new wonders in each work, but always there is something missing, something overlooked or scorned. It is this something that drives me on to continue the search. Giacometti once described it thusly: "In search of the impossible."

(Jack Kling)

COURTESY OF THE ARTIST. PHOTO I. SERISAWA.

Mantled Shore by Glen R. Bradshaw (b. 1922). 1959. Casein wash on rice paper.

Writing about my own painting always creates some uneasiness for me because my primary means of communication is visual rather than verbal. It is possible to write about work methods and overemphasize the "nuts and bolts" side of art, and it is just as easy to go to the other extreme and pay lip service to ideas that I think that I believe but which, to more objective eyes, seem remote from what my paintings actually reveal. With these extremes in mind, my comments must then be measured to some extent against the work itself, and, if there seems some discrepancy, I believe

that what the painting conveys should be regarded as nearer truth.

Among the beliefs that guide me are these: art requires order; the artist's work should reflect his uniqueness; the artist should know and respect the craft of painting; and a painting should be a rewarding visual experience for the viewer. I am aware that I prefer to work on absorbent paper, that I enjoy the immediacy of marks made with soft brushes and fluid paint, and that I often use complex color relationships.

My subject matter is nearly always lake-country landscape, but it is based on fundamental relationships and experiences rather than specific views.

Each painting is begun rapidly and intuitively, without preliminary studies, directly on rice paper. Then the relationships are compounded by the application of many overlays of thin casein paint. The work is continuously judged, and changed, until I feel that a precise unity of all its parts has been achieved.

How my work may or may not fit into current art style at any time is of little importance to me. It seems enough to do whatever I can, as well as I can, and to concentrate on the things which have meaning for me. Painting has meaning for me.

(Glen R. Bradshaw)

Red Horses by Harold M. Kramer (b. 1912). 1967. Latex wash on board. 18 x 22 inches.

Art is the act of creating an experience for both the viewer and the creating artist. The artist sees his meanings, his feeling-thinking, emerge from his work. This emergence from the canvas, paper, wax or clay is in accordance with the structuring he sets upon this art.

A major goal of the experimental artist is to select, invent or renovate a structuring that will house his idea-feelings. There are many, many structures in art and yet, in order to build them, he falls back on eight bricks — plastic or graphic means. These means are line, shape, form, color, value, pattern, texture, and sometimes movement. He may select two to eight of these bricks to build his creative structure, but in all cases he should be conscious of the restrictive and limiting nature of this art so as to expand it to his fullest use.

The mature artist can see-understand his work. His selection of structure, plastic means, and emotional idea gives him conviction and order. Without these, he tilts at windmills, deals with inconsistent emotions, and cancels out strength of meaning. The structural and graphic selections the artist makes do not confine his art but rather define and release it. The seeing-understanding of the wedding between his emotional ideas and his means is one of the purest profits in art. It is the meaning of the first line, when I said, "art is the act of creating an experience for both the viewer and the creative artist."

Art is not the act of locking nature into the canvas; this is merely depicting real estate. Art is man-made nature, and the understanding of the nature, its structure, plastic means, and energies wedded to an emotional idea.

(Harold M. Kramer)

White Line Landscape by Keith Crown (b. 1918). 1966. Watercolor. 22 x 30 inches.

The droplet of color running down the paper, the gathering of water and color in the valleys of warps, the confluence of saturated areas: these are natural, unforeseeable incidents of watercolor painting misjudged by some to be crude craftsmanship. To erase them would be to destroy the signs of adventure, to kill the painting.

One can discover only from a great deal of painting the delicate reactions of some colors placed in areas saturated by others, the sparkling whites of bare paper between areas of colors, the wild-fringed invasion of one color upon another when they are impinged, the power of scumbling and blotting. Without a subject, though, all of this is empty performance. The subject is all-important: it motivates the painting. Too bad it doesn't come in tubes — high-quality subject-motivation ground with the finest, most permanent ingredients — for the subject is so much more than a surface covered with bottles and apples, a landscape, a sailing vessel charging the waves. This subject-motivation is the personal observation, the poetry, the penetrating visual statement, the idea that pervades the picture, giving its appearance, its structure. Here one needs a certain kind of courage to ignore all that has gone before, that is so much surer of pleasing. With boldness reach into the painting with your brush to struggle with the unseen (the subject), and try to make it emerge into the visible.

(Keith Crown)

73

The Inward Sun by Elsa Warner (b. 1900). 1964. Acrylic wash and collage. 30 x 40 inches.

The immediacy of pleasure with the real, abstract moods of nature has been rewarding for me in the watercolor medium. The intuitive, spontaneous, imaginative, and automatic processes grow from the freedom of the activity of watercolor as it develops and shifts under the brush. This is an intimate and spiritual experience. The emerging images possess an emotional recall from many walks with nature in the cycles of her lights and seasons.

Abstract imagery, that which concentrates in itself the essential qualities of things, often reveals in depth their significance. My evolvement with inner and outer found images in collage activated the automatic juxtaposition of forms and colors. There is an intangible bond between the artist and his personal expression, and to these feelings I must add the joy of working in this infinitely challenging medium.

(Elsa Warner)

74

Message to Paul Klee by Olga Higgins. 1963. Watercolor and ink line.

The combination of watercolor, or casein, and working in line has long been a favorite approach of mine. Being an experimenter and innovator by nature has allowed me to move into many art fields and to employ media such as watercolor, Conté crayon, casein, gouache, collage, monotype, and oil. I am very prolific and work with great fervor, often producing a hundred paintings over a period of several months.

My most successful paintings occur when I am working on a specific series, sometimes concerned with subject but more often with media alone. When such a series is over, my evaluation of the work begins. Many times only a dozen may be saved, with the rest doomed to my "lemon bin"; but these discarded works may well supply me with collage material for future series.

The painting Message to Paul Klee *is a result of one such series that was devoted to line and watercolor wash.*

Today my greatest thrill as a painter springs from the memory of my long years as a commercial artist, which began at the age of 14. Having once experienced the pressures of deadlines, specifications, and a regimented life, I can now express myself with full freedom. Because of this, I feel a deepened sense of joy in my present creative endeavors.

(Olga Higgins)

Second Theme with a Double Subject by John W. McIvor (b. 1931). Watercolor.

I would like to tell you what I think watercolor is, except every time I nail an axiom in place it seems to rule out other things. What's worse, people armed with my own walls then fence me in and them out.

I've taught some sixteen courses of watercolor, but on the other hand I'm not sure I ever taught anyone its essence successfully; I think they learned this themselves. I taught them to be sensitive to transparency, white space, drawing, and the other things — but these other things that make up a watercolor are all media-wide, and this is where the art lies. It seems obvious, then, that watercolor is very personal and not categorical.

In 250 words I might sum up why watercolor for me isn't just a craft, but I couldn't in a thousand words define why it's an art. I guess, then, the category is that craft is craft and art is art, and craft is of little comfort to me. When I'm fortunate, I sometimes can define the other with a painting.

(John W. McIvor)

Utah Red Cliff by Alexander Nepote (b. 1913). 1957. Watercolor and collage on Masonite.

My reactions, which are embodied in my paintings, are the result of an intensive search: to see, as best I can, beyond the obvious to hidden deeper realities. I feel that man's existence in historical time is his greatest experience — his life. It is not my intention to describe a place but to suggest that the transitory things of nature are not the real reality. The ultimate reality is the never-ending process in which things come into being, exist, and pass away — the mystery of continuous change. This is a paradoxical situation, where the process which unfolds in historical time is the eternal, the absolute. To me, this constant transformation is best expressed by the illusion of deep space where relationships of light suggest the energy and movement in historical time, where mass and texture display the disruptions and marks of perpetual change. The esthetic fabric unites the seen and unseen, the known and felt, the specific and universal. In my paintings details of snow, cliffs, and crevices lead us to feel the spirit of massiveness, vastness or intimacy and to realize such experiences as aloneness, ambiguity, and mystery.

The technical process echoes the ultimate content. Torn pieces of thin black and white etching papers are glued to Masonite and painted as they are placed into position. There they are subjected to continuous modification — scrubbed, rubbed, pulled off, cut out, and new pieces added. The textured pieces (resulting from the tearing off process) are frequently reglued into the painting in different places, and repainted. This battle with materials continues until the work comes to life.

(Alexander Nepote)

THE DYNAMICS

OF THE MEDIUM

4

Dynamics: 1. The branch of mechanics that treats of the motion of bodies in space (kinematics) and the effects of forces in producing motion, and of the laws of the motion thus produced (kinetics): opposed to statics.

(Britannica World Language Dictionary)

The greatest concern, indeed the very crux of this entire volume, is contained in the deceptively routine area of dynamics. In no other area of art instruction has more misinformation been dispensed, with the result that it has served to inhibit rather than expand the artist's individual personality.

An over-concern with methodology is totally distracting when one is attempting to gain major goals involving content. Such things are attained through practice which builds experience, and technological solutions are then a wedding of common sense with that experience. It would be far more helpful to develop an understanding of the latitude that already exists and of the possibilities that beckon. The artist employing watercolor must be free to work as he sees fit: capriciously, meticulously, and, most important of all, independently! He cannot subscribe himself to a time element or a work pattern that is dictatorial. Popular formulae for "planning a watercolor" or "how to paint a tree" must be scuttled and relegated to that dismal level slightly above "painting by the numbers." Planning a painting is hardly the issue, for that is a most personal thing; but the true artist could never submit to another's method as a standard of procedure.

Nicolaides sums it up this way:

Do not try to learn a formula, but to become sensitive, to feel more deeply. Do not try to master a particular technique. Progress has been made by the people who refused to submit themselves to mediums. The rules of technique have been made by people who copied those who made the progress. You will paint well when you are able to forget that you are painting at all. When you are conscious of your medium, things become difficult, but when your interest is completely absorbed by the model — the idea — your materials become easier and easier to handle. Therefore, practice is the watchword.

Most artists recall nostalgically the use of the thumbnail or small preliminary sketch. In the early going, when sureness is a rare companion, such investigations are of reasonable value and comfort. Thumbnails in the hands of the mature artist may not only prove revealing, but worthy as individual efforts in themselves. As richly rewarding as they may be, it rarely follows that they

rush Drawing (opposite) by Jack Kling . 1929). 1967. Ink on board. 4 x 4 ches.

would be copied verbatim; this would produce a mechanical, warmed-over kind of art. The feeble argument which suggests that if you cannot follow your plan then you are less the artist is pure nonsense and was a source of great irritation to me in my art-student days.

To elaborate further, let us assume that an artist begins a painting that will presumably occupy him for several hours, or several days. Why should he, then, proceed to devote the bulk of his time to the embellishment of a thought resolved at the outset, when possibly no later than an hour or two after getting underway a worthier goal may be suggested? Does he not know the meaning of flexibility, and of its richness of reward? Is it not a further possibility for him to approach a painting wherein a newer thought or an accident or turning may be seized upon; or could he not abandon the total concept and begin anew if a more enticing challenge offered itself? All of this is in direct conflict with the method plan, in which hours of routine busywork are devoted to the coloring-in of frozen diagrams.

Perhaps through the recital of personal experiences, a more forceful note may be struck in this forlorn area. As a student member of a class that worked exclusively in watercolor (on landscape locations), I was instructed to paint the sky first. Many times a sky was painted again and again until the proper result was achieved; after this initial victory, the rest of the painting could begin. Oddly enough, at a neighboring art school a class of similar nature was being advised to paint the sky last! Since skies were relatively simple things to paint, and could be adjusted to the rest of the painting with little effort, this bit of fatuousness was judged helpful. The pity of it all, at least to me, was that these dubious lessons were given in sincere fashion by hardworking teachers who were capable painters. The fear, in retrospect, is that damage was done to young artists who subscribed to such naiveté.

Watercolor was not, is not, and will never be a "class" on location or in the studio, working from the still life or the figure. It is a medium, as are oil, pen and ink, or acrylic. Class titles such as "watercolor landscape" and "watercolor figure painting" are meaningless, and invariably inhibit the student. Furthermore, an artist who works in watercolor is not a "watercolorist" but a painter who employs the watercolor medium for myriad reasons, perhaps too numerous to recite. Traditional definitions of just what a watercolor is are rather unfortunate in themselves. Each sincere attempt is either obscured by technicalities or diluted by an over-reverence of tradition.

After all, watercolor is nothing more than a paint whose pigment is finely ground and suspended in an aqueous solution of gum arabic, and it is miscible in water! The Europeans, in order to distinguish it from opaque paints, refer to it as *aquarelle*. Purists have traditionally frowned upon the introduction of anything foreign to the transparent colors, specifically, opaque white. It was generally conceded that a very white (a *cream* color was acceptable on rare occasions) hand-made rag paper was the most effective support to use. The only point of real significance in all of this concerns the permanency of the medium. For the purist of yesterday and today may not have produced any work of consequence, but it will certainly endure. To quote from the noted authority, Ralph Mayer: "When permanent colors are used on pure rag water-color paper and the picture is kept under the same normal conditions of preservation as are accorded other objects of art, the technique is as permanent as any other."

Working on a glittering white surface is fundamental to artists employing practically all media. In this way alone, a maximum brilliance is obtained from the translucent nature of watercolor. If the artist selects another support, or a toned ground, he does so with the complete knowledge that he is abandoning luminosity to gain other qualities. He knows that when he gravitates from the pure white ground, he loses the high rate of refracted light that plays off of it and back through the films of color. But by employing watercolor, the artist is granted the inestimable gift of being able to get where he is going quickly, often with effective conclusion. Accidents are omnipresent, and are conscripted to lead the way to newer discoveries. There is an excitement in the act of painting that is often inherited by the viewer. There is an air of expectancy and thrill that comes with each new juxtaposition of color, form or line. The very nature of the paint consistency, plus the design of the brush, invites the artist to continue painting with infrequent refills from his palette. The ease of mixing, especially in the subtle world of tertiary color, contributes to the flow of uninterrupted spontaneity. Everything is directed toward and suited to the *alla prima* attitude, and all paths have been cleared for the inductive response. Still this has to be only one thought, one suggestion, albeit more sophisticated and intriguing to the contemporary painter.

The painter may change the support to cloth, add collage of white or color-fast papers; paint back over the collage, add ink, work with stick, twig or bamboo; use rubber cement as a frisket, or wax-resist, or invent his own approach. He may splash and splatter, or let the paint run; what does it matter if the floor is dirtied or his clothes are soiled? How does one think when such concerns are cluttering up the mind? Scrape the paint, scratch at it, scrub it away; ruin the surface and start again. Or sit quietly at a table and use rulers, T squares or any other mechanical device to gain the desired result. Break every rule, ignore all advice; but know it first! Only through long experience can one expect to grow, to understand and appreciate the singular beauty of watercolor. This medium is not simple to work with — but then, neither are the others; it is time that this be made abundantly clear. There is every good reason to believe that a great artist would be able to work in any medium, even one completely alien to his nature. Take from him all of his familiar and beloved materials, leave others in their place, and it will be a matter of time alone before great works will again pour from his studio. As an example, John Marin had great difficulty with his control of oil, particularly in the manipulation of the fluid calligraphy he excelled in; but, then, his watercolor paints were always near at hand. There are stories of the Mexican artist, Diego Rivera, who drew with shoe polish on newspaper all through the great depression of the thirties. At the expense of seeming redundant, it would be prudent if the aspiring artist learned to draw and compose; one could then assume that after these major victories, problems of materials and techniques would be easily conquered.

Because there has been so much said about how one should paint a watercolor, the following antidotal information has been included. The fullest control of a very fluid, water-miscible paint is maintained by varying the proportions of water and paint. For those encountering watercolor as an initial experience, it seems furtive, elusive, and downright unruly. Apprehensions soon vanish, however, after competence and confidence are gained, mainly through practice. When the artist works a relatively dry brush into a wet surface, he maintains a firm control of his stroke, as is virtually the case in all liqueous media. A dry brush applied to a dry surface or a wet-into-wet approach affords still other possibilities, and in this light the aspiring artist makes progress. We could discuss scraping, scratching, splattering or splashing in detail, but this would be antithetic to our premise. In addition to the obligation of the individual's personal experimentation with the medium, there are the works of thousands of other artists to be studied carefully and used as a fount of information if not inspiration. The paintings reproduced in this section alone provide a good beginning. One may quickly note the value of a wet or dry calligraphy, or the use of a stick to apply paint or a hard-edge instrument to scrape it away. There is little advantage to be gained in suggesting one kind of tool or another, since we could compile a list that would fill volumes, and they would all make a different mark. Splattering and dripping paint need to be done, more than to be described. The very heart of this adventure is imbedded within the hide of discovery, and is highly personal.

Painting is not without its amusing experiences; and those who are either blindly or platonically devoted to this medium in particular make bountiful contributions. For one thing, there is a breed of *artists* who take enormous pride in being able to produce a very narrow line or minute shape with their largest brush. They will use the same brush so exclusively that all of their results are similar. It has never occurred to them that they might well use a smaller brush for smaller strokes, and the larger brush for massive areas. There are those who will not put paint on their palettes; frugality is part of their composure, and their work shows it. A stumbling mass of insipid, unchromatic brush-stroking appears worn and faded at best. Another manifestation of frugality is seen when a large mass is to be painted, and only a minimum paint mixture is prepared. While this is common to most neophytes in all media, it is devastating in watercolor, since it is time-consuming to duplicate color mixtures in general, and time is often a vital factor.

The paintings that have been carefully selected for reproduction in this section possess a strict, singular purpose. They are not intended to entertain or amuse, but to be inquired into, dissected, and laid open. We want to know why and how the artist performed as he did, even when he may not be able to explain the nature of his automatic responses. The professional painter, along with experts in other fields of endeavor, creates in a relatively subconscious way. Excellent drivers, after arriving at their destinations, often forget the paths they took. If one were to ask a pianist, a surgeon, and a golfer precisely how they achieve their high level of performance, they would probably be quite unable to provide totally clear explanations.

The professional painter is well equipped, and he comes by this through experience. He has long since ceased to blame his equipment for his failures or inadequacies, although it would be well to keep at a safe distance when a defective paint or support has been unwittingly employed. He knows what to reach for and generally where it is; his instincts tell him these things while his mind is saturated with deeper concerns. And this applies to the action painter as well as the deliberate mechanic. We will look at the paintings contained in this section with this in mind, and try to get inside of the individual artist to determine why he resorted to a given approach. By the use of photo-enlargement, we will journey with the artist down a very private road. Here is a truly magical experience in any painter's medium, for all have their unique qualities that allure and, sometimes, seduce. Rather than be awe-struck or bewildered by these microscopic adventures (for such things are inordinately delightful), we will be engaged in a private autopsy of *why* and *how* an artist speaks.

One last word before turning to the paintings. Although they have been selected solely on the basis of their individual ability to project a clear message relative to the dynamics of watercolor, they are quite properly, in their own right, superb paintings by accomplished artists. These people have been most generous in allowing me the privilege of presenting their work in this manner. It would be safe to assume that they share with me the belief that watercolor is capable of inimitable expressiveness and unsurpassed beauty.

Page from Shelter Sketchbook by Henry Moore (b. 1898). 1941. Watercolor, ink gouache.

The pictorial essay of this section is mainly concerned with the exposition of the watercolor medium in all its forms, clarified by an accompanying enlarged detail of each work. However, with the paintings of Georgia O'Keeffe and Morris Graves it was not deemed necessary to include the detail, but rather to display the work as large as possible. Biographical data is kept to a minimum; the text is devoted to a clinical examination of the work itself.

Evening Star, III by Georgia O'Keeffe (b. 1887). 1917. Watercolor on paper. 9 x 11⅞ inches.

This startling painting by the pioneer contemporary American painter Georgia O'Keeffe is even more remarkable when one realizes that it was executed in 1917. The bold simplicity of its structure virtually overwhelms the viewer, and relates to the reductive thinking so prevalent today. Unlike the present school, the O'Keeffe statement does not deny textural concerns, but instead welcomes such events with open arms. All artists know that well-thinned or liquid wash will produce unpredictable results when applied to various surfaces. In *Evening Star, III* we see the result of this phenomenon and its magnificent contribution to the broad, linear forms.

Bird (opposite) by Morris Graves (b. 1910). 1957. *Sumi.* 34 x 22¾ inches.

In Morris Graves' handsome *Bird* we witness a similar happening. But, rather than imprison the textural experience within the stroke, Graves has pre-wet the surface in order to encourage a flowing out, so to speak. With but one purpose in mind, namely, that of exploring the dynamics of the medium, it would seem foolhardy to attempt this magnificent performance in any other way. It must also be noted that the elusiveness purposely sought out in painting *Bird* is made valid primarily through Graves' acute sensitivity and competent draftsmanship.

COLLECTION OF THE MUSEUM OF MODERN ART, NEW YORK. MR. AND MRS. DONALD B. STRAUS FUND.

The Mirror by Edward Reep. 1956. Water-color on paper. 20½ x 28½ inches.

The primary objective in painting *The Mirror* was to set down my reaction to the bright yet elusive light patterns before me, in addition to the intriguing, shapeless, nocturnal forms of lake and island. There is the recollection of seeking to build a structure from inside, or center-to-outside. The insistent chandelier-like image was omnipresent, and there was an attempt to present this thought as an unfolding, not too unlike a Mercator map projection.

The broad scraping away of wet paint that fills this work is the obvious purpose for its inclusion. Painting on a bitter cold night by a park lake forced this approach upon me, as the paint refused to dry. As each scraping seemed to illuminate a new area, entangled light patterns appeared to glow from within the painted surface. This is an example of how the content-goal may dominate and dictate method.

COURTESY OF THE ARTIST. PHOTO I. SERISAWA.

Ancient Grass by Meredith Olson (b. 1929). 1961. Watercolor on paper. 26 x 40 inches.

This splendid painting offers much when carefully examined. However, from Miss Olson's own words, we realize that she is not nearly as conscious of her method as of her philosophical needs. She states the following: "In this nocturnal scene, I try to impart the experience of seeing the burnished grasses of summer as a symbol of the continuity of life through time. *Ancient Grass* is not the grass of one season, but is as old as man himself."

At the time *Ancient Grass* was painted, Miss Olson was deeply involved in a series of works based upon this premise. Her dependence upon the repeated scratching away of paper and paint, which is so well revealed in the detail, is quite understandable. For how else could she capture the spirit of a nocturnal grass, when limited to an essentially *dark-over-light* paint? A change of medium would solve the problem, but could never present the personal, inimitable answer seen here. The beauty of *Ancient Grass* is a direct result of a relentless pressure brought to bear upon old limitations.

87

Grouping by Irene Koch (b. 1929). 1957. Watercolor collage on paper.

The sheer feminine gracefulness of Irene Koch's *Grouping* is largely the result of her management of tumbling pattern-forms, but it is further emphasized by her brilliant tonal scale. It ranges from glistening lights to velvet darks, each note clearly in tune. The detail peers into hidden recesses of quick line and spontaneous wash, displaying the artful manner in which complete and confident authority dominates her work.

Torn entries of other painted surfaces are so skillfully fused that one is hardly aware of their inclusion. The fortuitous rewards of this collage (technically, découpage) may be noted, as varied textures and movements are rudely imprisoned and placed into newer orbits. *Grouping* epitomizes a realm of eternal elegance.

Untitled by Matsumi Kanemitsu (b. 1922). 1967. Ink wash on paper. 15 x 17½ inches.

By far the most reductive or minimal statement to be shown in this section is this painting by Matsumi Kanemitsu. It was produced as one of a series of experiments with ink and wash on paper, which was often cut apart and remounted on new surfaces. *Untitled,* however, is on a single surface, although the drifting patterns to the left suggest another material.

The enlarged detail readily demonstrates that there is more lurking within this simple yet powerful statement than first meets the eye. While a shimmering force appears half-coiled and ready to strike, we are allowed to examine its hide and anatomy. This method of ink and wash application, which is ultimately washed away, leaving only stained patterns on the paper's surface, is most effective, and the results are highly unpredictable. Kanemitsu readily confesses that he discovers as he goes, yet the viewer senses that he is in full control of his search.

COLLECTION OF EDWARD REEP.

89

COURTESY OF THE ARTIST. PHOTO I. SERISAWA.

Beach by Harold Kramer (b. 1912). 1967. Latex wash on board. 17¼ x 22 inches.

The superb graphic controls and confident draftsmanship exhibited in this vibrant statement do much to simplify our earlier thesis regarding the importance of the artist's background or training. Certainly the method involved here is far from complex, and that is a great part of the painting's pristine beauty.

What dignifies Kramer's wash and line comes through years of creative explora-tion. He exaggerates form and rearranges it into multiple station points, but above all he gives it further meaning through a personal symbology. His explicit line meanders about or it digs out an incisive shape; it may be wide or narrow, or autonomously awkward. There is a playing of all this against a pattern of striated wash, to the accompaniment of other inventive shape-symbols. The enlarged detail attests to this and more, especially with the discovery of both sharp and furry line. Rarely is the viewer presented with a more abundant world of pure visual delight than in this joyous painting.

1,000 Watercolor Touches by John W. McIvor (b. 1931). 1967. Watercolor on paper.

McIvor is neither a slave to tradition nor does he fret over the moral issue of eclecticism. The detail reveals all; the artist's brush moves confidently over the surface, dripping, scraping, scoring, yet always in touch with and seeking his goal. Imbedded in the larger and more obvious movements are countless smaller, startling thrustings, deepening dimension as well as bearing the sure mark of the draftsman.

It is important for me to work with materials which can be manipulated quickly and precisely. Not that I always work with a great rush, but when ideas do occur at a quickened meter, I demand a material which responds fast so the form can be built while it is still clear in my mind. With other media, I have experienced, at times, the painting seemingly dying in the process of being built; the work was lost in the gap between inception and realization — the "credibility gap."

(John W. McIvor)

COLLECTION OF THE ARTIST. PHOTO FREDERIC MARSCHALL.

Horizontal Still-Life by Jo Rebert (b. 1915). 1962. Watercolor on paper. 27 x 40 inches.

Rarely are we treated to the sparkling beauty of the uncluttered transparent watercolor as with the work of Jo Rebert. While this sensitive colorist paints in many other media, *Horizontal Still-Life* has been carefully selected for its mastery of the glazed wash.

Jo Rebert is an exquisite composer, especially when involved with chromatic energy. Her work may be fully appreciated only when viewed in color. She not only maintains a seemingly effortless structural dominance in her work, but also relies upon the accidental overlappings of color to secure patterns in place and to provide deeper dimensions to her orchestration. In the artist's own words, "Watercolor lends itself to a rapid flow of ideas because it can be so rapidly and easily destroyed." This firm control over a spontaneous, transient surface is evident in both the painting and its detail.

6 P.M. Glow, June by N. P. Brigante (b. 1895). 1965. Watercolor and ink on paper. 24 x 36 inches.

The singular beauty of Nick Brigante's space-world is breathtaking to behold. When seen magnified, it is overwhelming. *6 P.M. Glow, June* is only one of a long series that has intrigued not only Brigante, but his followers as well. There is a mastery of medium that can result only from long experience, and there is a wedding of performance with the philosophical directives of *Yang* and *Yin* that is equally impressive.

Brigante displays alternate patterns of wet line into wet and dry surface, and dry brush over wet and dry surface. He offers a multitude of textures that swarm through and about the painting, adding emphasis to his adroit use of scale and transposition. At first we are only witness to a ceaseless drama, but soon we are drawn introspectively into Brigante's world and become a part of it.

COLLECTION OF LYTTON SAVINGS AND LOAN ASSOCIATION. PHOTO BOB FORESTER.

COLLECTION OF I. SERISAWA. PHOTO I. SERISAWA.

Formulations by Hilda Levy. 1954. Watercolor and ink on "hospital paper." 19½
x 19½ inches.

This bounteous work by Hilda Levy lies
a world apart from all others in this section. We are treated to the spectacle of a
massive, yet calligraphic, unrest, all pro-
foundly under the artist's control.

Essentially watercolor, ink line, and
wash on a textured paper, Mrs. Levy's
bold structure is the clue to the painting's
success. She has manipulated a sensitive
arrangement of textured shapes which ultimately plays against the complex linear
patterns. In this way the monochromatic
calligraphy stands forth or falls away at
the artist's will. There is an imposing
sense of scale and depth to be found in
this work, and the enlarged detail offers
a dramatic view of how this was achieved.

Demaphon #2 by Leonard Cutrow (b. 1911). 1963. Watercolor and ink on rice paper (mounted). 21¼ x 18¼ inches.

The exquisite management of the chiaroscuro in *Demaphon #2* is typical of Cutrow's dramatic *oeuvre*. There is resounding symphony heard here—one bursting with relentless fury that seems to engulf the viewer. Additionally, the detail reveals a particularly unique assortment of surface textures.

That so much power can be generated with watercolor wash, ink line, and rice paper seems astonishing at first, but we are soon provided with insights far removed from method and media. Massive washes sprawl over their more delicate counterparts, complex spatterings supply scale and vibration, and a broken, dotted line is omnipresent. Materials and artist are one, and there is little time for technical persuasion. What happens does so because of the careful preparation that has preceded this and countless other kindred efforts.

The Red Tear Drop by Leonard Edmondson (b. 1916). 1957. Watercolor collage on paper. 19½ x 28½ inches.

The patterned world of *The Red Tear Drop* is but one of a long series produced by Edmondson several years ago. It has lived in my memory, and was included in this section to display a rare use of the watercolor medium.

The patient attitude and obvious concern for a total synthesis is evident, but there is also a persistent, floating movement that denies complacency. There are echoes and dimensions that carry with them a myriad number of absorbing tactile sensations. This latter quality is most apparent in the enlarged detail, as is the painstaking care that went into its formulation. Edmondson relies heavily upon the transparent nature of watercolor to further enforce a sense of overlapping pattern, which in turn lends added emphasis to the painting's dimensional achievements.

96

South Side by Jerome Land (b. 1908). 1963. Watercolor and transparent plastic on black paper.

Perhaps the most eventful textural journey of this essay is found in the enterprising work of Jerome Land. Paint was initially applied to a wet, non-absorbent surface, to be eventually blotted with wrinkled, paint-saturated tissue. The support which Land employs is a transparent plastic material (polyethylene or cordite), which is mounted on black paper. He likens this to the effect of a large Kodachrome, except that a "black light" is utilized.

The resultant tonal qualities are de-pendent upon the support, as the trans-parent paint films that follow are affected by it. Land states that he finds in this method ". . . a great deal of flexibility in trying to attain a desired result. Shapes, textures, and tones can be richly realized to create moods of considerable depth and mystery."

There can be do doubting this com-ment by the artist. *South Side* is not only an impressive painting in its own right; it enhances our thesis by providing new and rewarding painting adventures. The enlarged detail is unbelievably generous in intimately exposing an all-too-often hidden fabric.

COLLECTION OF THE CALIFORNIA NATIONAL WATERCOLOR SOCIETY. PHOTO BOB FORESTER.

A CHRONOLOGY

The Bank. 1957. Watercolor and ink on cotton skrim cloth. 24 x 34 inches.

OF CHANGE

In any endeavor there is nothing more constant than change. There is, in fact, definite cause for alarm when change is absent. My own work in watercolor is presented here solely to illustrate this firm belief. Furthermore, it is evident by what we have already seen in the earlier sections of this book that there appears to be infinitely more variation in the melange of other artists' work, but this is only superficially true. For while we may play a Klee against a Grosz, or a Cézanne against a Homer, and note remarkable differences, visualize a Klee against a Klee and there is another interaction altogether.

In most instances change takes place without our knowing it; consciously forcing or seeking change carries no guarantee that it will happen. What remains clearly needful to me is the attempt to move (hopefully) forward. It is unlikely that a sensitive artist could assign such welcome movement to his own efforts, and this will not be the case here. The changes noted have more to do with philosophical attitudes, emotional or intuitive perception and, enigmatically enough, structuring that appears pragmatic in retrospect. But there will be no doubt as to motivation, and the message will be clear. It would be far less revealing to depend upon art critics, historians or any other second-hand source for this information.

Most of the work shown in this section covers an approximate period of twenty-one years — from 1946 until 1967. During that time, the bulk of my efforts was devoted to the watercolor medium, with occasional work executed in oil and lithography. Since 1958, the reverse has been true: virtually all of my paintings are either in oil or acrylic, with only infrequent returns to watercolor. Additionally, there has been an added emphasis on drawing and sculpture.

Most artists struggle to maintain a high level of quality, perhaps not in what they attempt or when they attempt it, but in what they will ultimately let out of their studios. In the exploration of new directions (which is another manifestation of change), it should be noted that for each promising gain there may also be a loss of ground. A frustrating yet natural phenomenon occurs when one produces work well ahead of oneself, at any given time. These and other factors contribute to the dilemma of the serious painter, and all this without a thought given to the concerns of critical acceptance. It would amaze the general public to discover how many paintings artists labor over diligently, to ultimately detest and destroy. Ivan Albright once confessed that he didn't really enjoy painting very much. He said, "I go at it the hard way, with my eyes wide open. But I do like getting the results I want. I'd rather paint one good picture than a hundred bad ones. Anybody can paint bad ones, including me."

To get away from oneself, to stand off and recognize weaknesses and to be able to do something about them — that is important! For example, just two years ago it became necessary for me to abandon all painting and draw for a solid year. Prior to that, my lack of knowledge and experience in three-dimensional form had gnawed away at me from within, the result being that for a full year my efforts were confined to sculpture. While the results were not always satisfying, the experience was invaluable.

Rarely, despite beckoning nostalgia, does one peer into the frozen past with a sense of great expectation. It is impossible for me to look back without seeing flaws, omissions, and futility. Rules and regulations based mainly upon craft or technique saturated my mind and limited my vision. Needless to say, this hapless condition did not appear so at the time, for even in ignorance there is unlimited joy. How does one know when training, environment, and exposure are narrow and confined? The teachings of the modern schools were not only ignored, but for the main unknown by my teachers. The Bauhaus was either pure fiction or merely tolerated. Expression outside of my little world was an impossibility, and what made matters worse was my inability to recognize this fact.

After two years of army service, my career took a sudden turn. Commissioned as an artist-correspondent under the auspices of the War Department, I came into contact with men such as Reginald Marsh, Mitchell Siporin, and a host of other renowned artists. Being with these men and seeing what they did and how they thought was a revelation. My own inadequacies came into focus with embarrassing regularity. Until then, drawing meant copying what was before me, and composition meant little more than arrangement. What a shock to find that other artists cared little for or completely ignored what seemed so sacred to me. And what pure joy to be released from the world of modeling to gain form or from the sole reliance of the "s" shape movement of the Renaissance.

Here and there was a breakthrough or an overcoming of the deep-seated concerns of ineptness. Color was always a love of mine, and while there had been severe and restrictive rules laid before me during my art-school tenure, it seemed far simpler to dispense with these than the others. There is no doubt that the war-artist experiences changed my entire perspective, philosophically as well as artistically. For while most of my work was of a documentary nature, something of deeper import was being included. Being awarded a Guggenheim Fellowship on the basis of paintings executed during the Italian Campaign was a thrilling experience. However, upon my return to America, with confidence and eagerness to get to work on proposed projects, further frustrations appeared. Grandiose ideas vanished one by one, as it was impossible to set down that which lived in my heart and mind. The war had sickened me, the futility of it was omnipresent, and once again my work appeared inadequate. Turning to numerous preliminary sketches, and in many instances full-scale black and white drawings, was my salvation. Each of these elaborate drawings took several days to complete. If the human figure were to appear, separate drawings would be made to further assure a result.

When the war experiences began to fade, there were other excitements to be found in both new and neglected areas, such as reading and studying in the worlds away from art. Teaching anatomy became a form of self-abuse that seemed imperative to me; after two years of it, condyles and tendons appeared everywhere, and that was enough. The most intelligent move at that time was to quit teaching at the school that was perpetuating beliefs that no longer held any meaning for me. Soon after, my teaching career resumed at the Chouinard Art Institute, and has continued to this day.

At Chouinard it became my great privilege to work with men of exceptional abilities, not only as artists but as master teachers: men such as Donald Graham, Herbert Jepson, William Moore, Watson Cross, and Harold Kramer, to name but a few. It is surprising how much one can absorb by simply working alongside fine teachers, especially when the core of instruction is built of creativity and not methodology. Concurrently, in 1950, it was my added pleasure to work with an artist of rare and separate nature. This was E. J. Bisttram, whose work was largely based upon the lessons of Dynamic Symmetry. An abstract painter of unusual quality, Bisttram proved to be a warm friend and an unwitting teacher. With Bisttram came my first real appreciation of picture structure, largely through the fascinating study of Hambidge's essays on Dynamic Symmetry. For some time after that, most of my work was based upon the rigid precepts of this doctrine.

Hence, while the early years were unaware years, the desire to paint was strong enough to allow me to hold out; at this writing the most productive years are yet to come. Painting has taken on new meanings for me, some so personal and private that they cannot be explained. A beginning has been established, and there is liberation in that knowledge. The way has been cleared of questionable competitiveness, and production is all that matters now. If there is growth through deeper meaning, then a hint of progress is suggested. Too often, to return to the original thesis, *all* that seems present is change, and that is not enough in itself.

Rarely will the work reproduced herein be non-figurative, although some paintings will have departed strongly from the original premise. None can be labeled as experimental beyond a point, as this is not my wont, although more recent oils and acrylics have very often abandoned subject matter. When the subconscious or sensory experience wells so strong within me that all reference to objectivity must go, it is scuttled; yet there has always been a point of departure known and visible to me. If this phase proves to be nothing more than investigative, so much the better. There is an itching underneath my skin to return to watercolor, but when, and in what form, remain to be seen. The only certainty is that it will never be the same, for there would be little thrill in it for me. It is far more successful to dream of new work than to produce it; but what does it matter? The excitement and anticipation in *doing* is now uppermost in my mind. This leads me to the further thought that accomplishment is inexorably bound up with continual production.

The traditional congregations of young artists in Paris and New York, as well as most urban areas, bear other implications that are germane at this moment. Artists young and old need to compare viewpoints and share experiences, and while this autobiographically flavored essay is in no way to be construed as a blueprint for others, it serves as another basis for that comparison. It is resorted to somewhat reluctantly in order to amplify the pictorial document. If it will aid in underscoring the need for constant search and inquiry, it will have served its purpose. Lastly, if such exposure of intimate concerns interlaced with frustration and desire may cause others to gain reassurance in the reevaluation of their own directions, then there will be added merit to its inclusion.

Who knows what form painting will take a century from now, or what new discoveries will influence tomorrow's art world? The only safe prediction is that there will be change. But painting will always remain as painting, despite the innovations that will coexist alongside of it in home or gallery, office or museum. A painting is far too personal and private an experience to be replaced. It

Swamp Note. 1950. Watercolor on paper. 15 x 21 inches.

Rebirth (opposite). 1954. Watercolor on paper. 19½ x 28 inches.

The paintings in this section were not created for this essay, but instead were selected painstakingly from work done over the years. It is far more meaningful to note change in this manner, even if a perfect chronology is not always present. Since valid change rarely follows a time schedule, I have determined that this is the most effective and fitting approach.

The two paintings facing one another here were executed fully five years apart. It is obvious that identical shapes appear in both works, although in *Rebirth* much has been added. The tranquil nature of the earlier work has given way to turbulence, gained mostly by a drier, spattered approach. In *Rebirth* there is a story of has a life of its own. It is an experience for others to experience: an event of the mind and soul. It may mystify, tantalize, bewilder, or delight. There is a magic both in the doing and in the seeing; there is the moment and eternity. As Gautier wrote:

> All passes. Art alone
> Enduring stays to us:
> The Bust outlasts the throne, —
> The Coin, Tiberius.

fury and devastation, along with the omnipotent regenerative force of nature. The splintered tree also offers refuge for two birds huddled together. In *Swamp Note* the brittle winter trees play against the early-morning light patterns and their own reflections. All is peace and calm.

It would be convenient to state that these paintings differ because they seek separate esthetic goals, but this would be only partly true. At the time *Rebirth* was painted, I was largely involved with kinetics; that is to say, there was a constant searching for the *inner energy* of all things. It was my desire to express the condition of an internal life-force, and so a new examination of familiar subject matter took place. I even sought out things that would lend themselves to my goals, such as the shattered tree in *Rebirth*. One painting is not better or further advanced than the other, but each has its own message, and was investigative and fruitful when painted.

COLLECTION OF MR. AND MRS. RUBIN R. URETZKY. PHOTO DON GARBER.

A Pier Goes On and On. 1955. Watercolor on paper. 21 x 29 inches.

These two pages are devoted to four picture structures that were employed for a number of reasons. For example, in *A Pier Goes On and On* I was involved with a very static horizontal and vertical motif of architectural form and space. The durable nature of such things, despite superficial decomposition, was of prime importance at the time.

In retrospect, it is all too evident that spattering paint was particularly fascinating to me then. In this statement the spatial apertures were covered over in order to preserve their clear, unmolested nature. It seems curious to me that there is a small painting of the large painting worked onto a wall near the left border — for what purpose I cannot recall. There is a finality about this painting and its structure which serves us well in a comparison with the three other works pictured here.

COLLECTION OF MR. AND MRS. NORMAN TOKAR. PHOTO DON GARBER.

Long Beach Pike. 1946. Watercolor on paper. 26 x 36 inches.

Painted immediately after World War II, *Long Beach Pike* was possibly my first effort in watercolor to successfully encompass distortion and animation. The joyous nature of all of my work at the time undoubtedly was a reaction to the preceding years of military service and to the paintings done then that spoke mainly of sadness and tragedy.

Long Beach Pike was initially painted on location, then done again, and much larger, in the studio. This second painting was carefully planned and completed in two or three days. It attempts to capture the colorful spirit of an amusement area as it might be seen through the eyes of children. The clouds form animal-like shapes and everything moves in tilted, muddled gaiety. There is a continuous writhing of colors, textures, and shapes which attempts to re-establish the cacophony of Pike sounds.

COLLECTION OF COLE OF CALIFORNIA.

Moon Story. 1954. Watercolor on paper. 27½ x 19¾ inches.

Somewhat architectural, with patterns continuing on to move through one another, *Moon Story* reveals the functioning of floating forms. There is a definite attempt to isolate as many shapes as possible without letting them overlap. When this is not feasible, smaller floating patterns are placed within larger shapes.

Moon Story was painted when timelessness was all-consuming to me. The intention was to invite, suggest, and provoke individual excursions. The gentle yet persuasive lunar magnetism and its resultant chiaroscuro was a source of great intrigue to me. Although *Moon Story* has only a murmuring voice, it has long been a favorite of mine.

COLLECTION OF THE ARTIST. PHOTO I. SERISAWA.

Still-Life with Apple #1. 1953. Watercolor on paper. 19¼ x 28½ inches.

This carefully planned work was painted soon after my friendship with E. J. Bisttram was formed. The lessons of Dynamic Symmetry that intrigued Bisttram were uppermost in my mind, and there was a concerted effort to develop structural authority in my work. Everything done at the time was ordered under the precise rules of root rectangles. In essence, these rectangular formats provide for proportionate orders of forms, shapes, angles, and thrusts.

In *Still-Life with Apple #1,* the opposing diagonals are quite obvious, but there is added interest contained in the transposition of dark and light. The immaculateness of the washes, as shown here, seemed vital at the time, but they ultimately displeased me and led to the spattering previously discussed.

COLLECTION OF NELBERT CHOUINARD. PHOTO DON GARBER.

Note. 1957. Watercolor and ink on cotton skrim cloth. 21½ x 34 inches.

Return to the Earth. 1953. Watercolor on paper. 19 x 28¼ inches.

Wind Bouquet (opposite). 1958. Watercolor and ink on cotton skrim cloth. 24½ x 34 inches.

The paintings *Note* and *Wind Bouquet* are drawn from a year-long period when all of my work was executed on a cotton skrim cloth backed with polyethylene. Given to me by a friend for experimental purposes, it provided an altogether new surface experience. The cloth was so widely woven that it proved to be semi-transparent, and practically invited collage to be placed under, or behind, the paint washes. When this was done, the warp and woof of the cloth fibers were accentuated, as if by dioramic means. The effect may be clearly seen in *The Bank,* shown on page 98.

With this work came a total abandonment of preparation for each painting; nor was any preliminary drawing done on the surface itself. In this spirit over 70 works were completed, but less than 30 were framed. My own desire was to capture an essence, spirit or condition, and consistent with this goal was the de-emphasis of subject. My thinking had now become less analytical and far more inductive.

Return to the Earth, completely out of chronological order, assumes a very important role when related to *Note,* shown just above it. It is an elaborate painting, and a most unusual watercolor, since it took over three days to complete. The striation of everything — earth, sky, architecture, and trees — was done in order to express a transitory step in the death of

COLLECTION OF MR. AND MRS. EDWARD BROIDA.

COURTESY OF PHYLLIS BRUHN. PHOTO DON GARBER.

a tiny settlement. These modest houses were put together with second-hand material, perspiration, and love, and they were doomed by the usurpation of a major-league ball park. Everything was headed back to whence it came.

Note was completed in little more than 45 minutes, yet it remains one of the most successful of the cloth watercolors. Its content-goal is distinct from that of *Return to the Earth*; consequently, it was executed in a different manner. But what of the time element — 45 minutes and three days! Prolific painters, writers, and composers often crank out work according to a time schedule, but its quality is highly debatable. It is here that I take issue with the automatic methods that produce inferior results.

One further point concerning change, or new events, is shown by the paint-runs in all three of these paintings. This innovation was a brisk step away from the earlier work, which was complete and immaculate. But the condition of the moment, and how to get the viewer to participate in the excitement felt in the very act of painting, were what I now considered vital.

COLLECTION OF KATHERINE PAGE PORTER. PHOTO I. SERISAWA.

Day in Echo Park. 1954. Watercolor on paper. 19 x 28½ inches.

Mountain. 1949. Watercolor on paper. 27½ x 20 inches.

COLLECTION OF WESTSIDE JEWISH COMMUNITY CENTER.

COURTESY OF MR. AND MRS. SIMON KORACH.

The Beach. 1950. Watercolor on paper. 21 x 30 inches.

108

Crystalware in Pink. 1954. Watercolor on paper. 20 x 28½ inches.

Crystalware in Brown. 1954. Watercolor on paper. 18½ x 28 inches.

Of the paintings on the opposite page, *Mountain* and *The Beach* represent a continuing interest in the dynamic structure already discussed. The resolute diagonals still remain, but there is a definite lessening of complete dependence upon them, and slight texturing has been added. *Day in Echo Park* completely abandons the angular format, although the circular patterns that appear did not constitute a trend. These patterns are peculiar to this painting alone, and spring from the spheroidal sun, the flora and their reflections. The lessons of Dynamic Symmetry had been effective, so much so that now there seemed to be an overemphasis given to structural order.

The two *Crystalware* paintings are deeply significant for me. *Crystalware in Pink* was painted first, and, apart from the esthetic goals that were sought, is a small tribute to those craftsmen who do such exquisite things with glass. This seeming irrelevancy is mentioned because such extreme beauty in man-made things, as well as nature, is very often a source of inspiration to the painter. But of greater importance to this chronicle of change is the further relinquishing of the extremely tight controls that had dominated my work thus far.

By the time *Crystalware in Brown* was begun, there were more important things to consider; despite all of my previous efforts to extract newer and richer meanings, the similarity of my works was haunting me. Determined to continue in watercolor, I was bothered because 99 percent of watercolor was applied to a white surface; hence *all* applied color had to be *dark over light.* In *Crystalware in Brown* there was a bold attempt on my part to reverse this procedure and allow light forms to move out of a dark periphery. Inspired by this new (to me) development, I began to make more purposeful selection of subject and shape; and this painting in particular became the precursor of eventual liberation.

COLLECTION OF DR. AND MRS. DONALD HULL.

COLLECTION OF MR. JACK JEANS.

World in World. 1958. Watercolor on paper. 21 x 29 inches.

Although it appears to be completely out of step, *World in World* was actually painted a year after the far more spontaneous cloth series. This only underscores my contention that while an artist's methods and materials may change radically, his basic loves remain the same. Apropos, there can be no questioning my proclivity for detailed order, for here it is again!

However, there is now more being said through less, and there is added opportunity for the viewer to read other highly personal meanings into the work. *World in World* projects my reflection in the window of a building housing a beach carrousel. It nostalgically recalls early interests both of boyhood and of painting. The *range* of time has now invaded my thinking, a range that may be concerned with the past, present or future, the infinite or momentary.

Windowed Microcosm. 1967. Watercolor découpage on board. 14½ x 12 inches.

Although painted much later than *World in World, Windowed Microcosm* is similar in many respects. There has been no conscious effort to create a smaller but magnified panorama within a larger one, yet this seems to have happened. One is reminded of the ground glass of the reflex camera, and of the small magnifying viewer used for more accurate focusing.

Windowed Microcosm is a découpage or collage of painted papers. The second of a series, it represents an excursion for me as well as the viewer; there is no goal in mind at the outset. New directions are suggested and even dictated by this method of tearing, cutting, and pasting translucent pieces of painted rice paper onto the paint surface, although they often lead to disaster. There has been an undeniable transformation of past methods and philosophical attitudes.

Subaqueous. 1967. Watercolor and ink on rice paper. 11½ x 17½ inches.

Euphony (opposite). 1967. Watercolor and ink on rice paper. 18 x 24 inches.

The two paintings shown here form the beginning of a pictorial summary. Both propose buoyant and introspective journeys; *Euphony,* opposite, suggests particular philosophical goals.

The group of paintings beginning on these two pages constitutes the last movement or alteration to be examined in this section. These later works were executed on a very fragile Japanese sketching paper (rice paper). Since it will tear or disintegrate easily when abused, overworking the surface is practically impossible.

These rice-paper paintings are relatively small, the largest being *Euphony* (18 x 24 inches), and were for the most part based upon numerous sketches completed on location, away from the studio. Working in this manner holds many meanings for me, not the least of which is the fullest enjoyment in the act of doing. As Fyodor Dostoievski once noted, the only goal of mankind lies in the process of attaining and not in the thing to be attained.

It would be presumptuous for me to refer to pictorial change here as more than a mutation or subtle shifting away from previous attempts, but what may be detected readily is a complete reversal of procedure. If the earlier *Crystalware in Brown* (page 109) was a "precursor of eventual liberation," then these paintings form a part of that new freedom.

Subaqueous was begun in the studio, with discovery alone in mind. (This painting and the two *Sun* paintings on page 115 are unusual in that they were not motivated by location sketches as were most of the paintings done in this series.) Old mannerisms appear, as if in an uncontrollable dream sequence. In *Subaqueous,* the almond shapes moving through a familiarly structured world are old loves, although they are far more resplendent than before. *Euphony* was drawn from a tortured segment of marine metal which ultimately suggested winglike shapes, ascension, and human life.

Shoot First. 1967. Watercolor and ink on
rice paper. 16 x 12 inches.

COLLECTION OF THE ARTIST. PHOTO I. SERISAWA.

COLLECTION OF THE ARTIST. PHOTO I. SERISAWA.

Sun Horizon #1. 1967. Watercolor and ink on rice paper. 12 x 18 inches.

Sun Horizon #2. 1967. Watercolor and ink on rice paper. 18 x 24½ inches.

While definitely a technical part of this series, *Shoot First* is philosophically disparate. It is one of a group of small paintings that allude to our trigger-happy society. It was begun at a waterfront shooting gallery, where all comers are invited to take pot-shots at clay pipes, eagles, rabbits, deer, and various other targets.

The two *Sun* paintings on the left are largely the product of a very old device. In this instance, however, the approach was far from being predetermined, and was born of utter frustration. I was working on several layers of rice paper, and the washes and ink lines bled through to form strange new patterns on the paper underneath. Each time a painting was removed, there was the beginning of another waiting below. Soon, and especially when the first results were abortive, there was a sense of delightful anticipation in this act; needless to say, the second and third attempts were often superior to the original statement. The two paintings are offered mainly to give broader substance to the works on the preceding pages, for in final form, despite a different approach, they vary little in treatment.

If the viewer finds subject matter in the *Sun* paintings, it will have to be attributed to his personal responsiveness. Both works, along with the titles bestowed subsequently, are merely triggers to the event. While hardly innovational, it represents the beginning of a different approach for the artist — different technically and philosophically.

To present more elaborate descriptions of these paintings would only defeat our purpose. I have only attempted to explain something of the manner in which they were realized and how they relate to this chronology of change.

115

Stairway to Yesterday. 1957. Watercolor on paper. 21 x 29 inches.

Stairway to Yesterday is based upon the identical theme that prompted *Return to the Earth* (page 106), even though the structure is dissimilar. When old replaces new, and especially when homes are torn down, nostalgia pervades the atmosphere. In this painting we discover the lonely surviving portion of a home — a street-level concrete stairway — posed against a barren plateau where the house once stood.

I have attempted a brief documentation of technical and philosophical change, all expressed through a single medium. To my knowledge, none of the artists whose painting appears in this book works exclusively in watercolor. Obviously, far more variety would be seen if their oils, graphics, and drawings were included, and this is particularly true of my own work. The point to be stressed, however, is that change is necessary; the amount or degree of it is not what matters.

This section opened with the statement that there would be "cause for alarm" if no change were evident in one's efforts; thus, the pictures that followed were selected carefully, with that consideration uppermost in mind. To change only one's medium may prove rewarding but is not in itself enough. Merely moving from one medium to another cannot be equated with the vast new adventures awaiting the artist when his efforts reflect and harmonize with the inevitable physical, emotional, and intellectual transformations he experiences throughout his life. Picasso declared pointedly that the *search* means nothing in painting, and that *to find* is the thing. Perhaps it is true that young artists are constantly searching, and the finding follows. But whatever the nature of the change, there is no standing still!

RELATED AND OTHER

Allegory by Kenneth Callahan (b. 1906). Tempera. 24 x 32 inches.

WATER-SOLUBLE MEDIA

In our time art accepts no boundaries. Fashionable art movements often seem to be more the creation of critics than of artists, a somewhat frantic attempt to create some kind of order out of the exciting chaos of today's art scene. In technique, too, the artists have stepped across traditional boundaries with the coming of plastics, metals, and the multitude of new products. The situation is extremely confusing for a person inclined to divide works of art according to the media employed.

Should the new acrylic paints, with properties very different from those of oils, be classified as oils? In what category is a drawing filled with painting or a painting filled with drawing? At what precise point does a collage become an assemblage? These questions which have plagued many an art jury over the years have become virtually meaningless. An artist may choose to work in any medium in which his idea can successfully be carried out.

(Dr. Thomas W. Leavitt, Director, Santa Barbara Museum of Art)

While we are primarily concerned with painting in transparent watercolor, it must be noted that there are many other water-base paints manufactured for sale and privately compounded that are termed watercolor. One year, while I was preparing a lecture for the Los Angeles County Museum, it became necessary to survey the current exhibition which was to be the basis for my talk. Among the juried paintings selected for showing, which had been extracted from thousands of entries, were no less than fifteen categories of watercolors. Among them were: egg tempera on board, gouache on Masonite, casein on wallboard, tempera on Upson board, and watercolor on paper. Without any reference to surface or ground, there also appeared, listed thusly: watercolor, casein, collage-watercolor, watercolor-gouache, and tempera-wax. There were countless other combinations and definitions among the far more numerous rejections, all carefully noted by the individual artist.

Before going any further, let me make it abundantly clear that what will be presented here is not to be mistaken for a scientific treatise. Rather than lay down rules, explore chemistry in paint, or in other manner pose as an authority in so complex an area, my sole purpose is to present a very basic explanation of water-soluble paint to the reader. For if the artist is going to explore and expand his dimensions as he goes, he must be aware of the physical properties of his paints and supports. In this manner he insures his work against deterioration or impermanency. But any deeper investigation additional to private experimentation should be undertaken by consulting reputable publications that deal exclusively with such things as materials and methods.

While it may seem perplexing to some that many of the aforementioned media appear very similar in character, there exist subtle differences in chemistry and manipulation that establish unique appeals to artists. For example, in addition to the broad definition of the traditional tempera medium, you will discover, when consulting a volume devoted exclusively to materials and methods, detailed treatises on such standard variations as egg tempera, gum tempera, soap tempera, and varnished and unvarnished tempera. Casein, gouache, and transparent watercolor will be looked at with the passionate dedication of the chemist, and the many glues and emulsions (wax, gum, natural, or synthetic) will be explained. Mixed techniques, along with the newly manufactured products in this as well as other areas, are presented with reliability, allowing the painter many options when formulating his own paint. Synthetic paints are elaborately described, the most popular being polymer tempera or acrylic. This astonishing paint is ground in water, mixes and thins with water, yet cannot be dissolved once it has dried thoroughly. The artist must gain complete understanding of the nature of synthetics, for while the polymer tempera colors are non-inflammable and non-toxic, this is not always so with other synthetics. We are not concerned with and therefore will not provide descriptions of paint that is not water-based, but it should be noted that acrylic-resin, ethyl-silicate, vinyl-acetate, and pyroxylin colors (lacquer) are also classified as synthetics.

Manufacturers are always alert to the needs of artists, often solving vexing problems for them. One example of this is to be found in the recent production of canvas primed with acrylic paint, the purpose being to accommodate both oil and water-base colors. While one may paint oil over a water-base paint, it is not advisable to apply water-base paint over oil.

GOUACHE

The most intimate relative of the transparent watercolor family is gouache. Artists and technicians alike have never been able to agree upon a single or precise definition of this elusive medium, but my description would read as follows: "A paint that produces delicate, luminous, high-key, and semi-transparent qualities." But let me hasten to add that gouache colors are essentially opaque, and only in the manipulation of overlapping brush strokes and washes does the semi-transparent quality delightfully appear. As in most media, however, the artist will dilute or thin his color to gain transparency, whether by accident or intent. All this seems more than proper to me, since painters employing gouache are predominately concerned with *alla-prima* qualities couched in a soft and reflective world.

Although gouache colors are manufactured and offered on the retail market, one must be extremely careful to select only those brands guaranteed to be permanent. Watercolors, watercolor inks, designers' colors, and gouache have been manufactured for use in the commercial advertising-illustration fields as well as for the easel painter. Some of these colors are exceptionally brilliant in hue, hence extremely inviting to use, but since there is little need for permanency in the commercial world, they are all too often *fugitive* or impermanent. My own attempts with gouache (that is, my version of gouache) have been executed with the addition of a good opaque white mixed into transparent watercolor; some artists gain an even more delicate result with the use of the less opaque Chinese white.

Concerning the working surface for gouache colors, there is one major difference that distinguishes them from the white-ground support desired for transparent watercolor. It is generally agreed that with an essentially opaque paint such as gouache there is little need for the refraction of light off the ground and through the color. Therefore, toned grounds are generally preferred, although there is no real objection to white or other high-key supports. The primary purpose of the toned ground is to enhance lighter masses and calligraphy. The supports usually preferred are cardboard, paper, cloth, and a multitude of specially prepared surfaces designed to attain highly personal goals. Cheap cardboards are often of such subtle and neutral nature that they have been widely used for gouache grounds. They are additionally attractive to painters since they require little or no preparation.

TEMPERA

The broad category of tempera must of necessity be broken down into some simplified form or we could easily devote a full section to it. This medium has enormous range, being involved with both oil and water-base colors. In the latter vein we will cover tempera, casein tempera, tempera-wax (or gum), and egg tempera only, as these are the most popular and widely used. When one considers that tempera colors may be formulated with either casein, gum, oil, wax, or egg, plus combinations of these elements, it becomes clear that there is a delightful experience awaiting the artist.

Tempera colors are classified as emulsions, which means that they are a mixture of oil, fat, resin or wax with water. The emulsion provides a heavier and more opaque base than found in transparent watercolor. When combined with a more coarsely ground pigment, tempera becomes very opaque in nature. At times you may note the classification of *oil-tempera* used, which indicates that an oily or fatty emulsion was present. If, however, you eliminate the fatty content and mix tempera with glue only, the result may now be termed *distemper*. In any event, tempera colors are noted for their resplendently luminous and sparkling qualities. They are most successfully applied to a rigid support that has been coated with gesso, which is a chalk or whiting mixed with glue, gelatin or casein. Tempera is virtually insoluble in water when dry and may be overpainted without great fear of moving the undercolor. Supports most commonly used are wood, untempered Masonite, and wallboards composed of various materials and structures. Although the common casein wall paint that has become so widely accepted in recent years may be used with success when preparing any of these panels, gesso remains unexcelled as a ground. Perhaps this is because it may be shaped or textured during application.

CASEIN TEMPERA

Apart from the popular acrylic colors, which are relatively new, casein tempera has enjoyed by far the widest use of all the opaque watercolors. This is mainly the result of its markedly simple formulation, plus the fact that nearly all well-known paint manufacturers offer it in virtually every hue and in convenient tubes. It was once very difficult to tube and keep casein tempera in working condition, but new discoveries and materials have conquered these problems. Enigmatically, casein colors have not received the stamp of full approval by all of the leading authorities; yet none of my own work in this area (some of it dating back twenty-five years) has seemed to discolor, fade or deteriorate.

Casein is extracted from skim milk which has been allowed to sour. The resultant fresh white curd is used as a binder or glue, and it is extremely effective, owning superior adhesive properties. Among the attractive advantages of casein is its ability to set up and remain impervious to water when dry. This enables the artist to rework an area without fear of lifting the undercolor. It also permits effective glazing and increases the painting's resistance to damage from moisture. Casein white, a most brilliant and effective color possessing enormous hiding power, has been largely responsible for the advances made with the underpainting white (controlled or quick-drying white) of the oil palette.

WAX AND GUM TEMPERA

The most brilliant color of all may well be found in paintings employing wax emulsions. Tempera wax will as a rule be formulated with a clean, white beeswax, but it is not to be confused with wax-encaustic or *hot wax*. The use of a wax emulsion provides the final work with excellent protection against moisture deterioration. As noted earlier, wax-encaustic was utilized by the Romans of ancient times for identical purposes. Various lusters may be obtained in lieu of varnishing by rubbing over the finished work with a soft cloth; but one must gain a working knowledge of this procedure through personal experimentation. Gum temperas are confected with emulsions consisting largely of either gum arabic, cherry gum, or gum Senegal. Their chief advantage is that they are extremely compatible both in mixing and formulation. Artists have been known to use gum arabic since earliest times, and have been well aware of its vital function as an adhesive in the transparent watercolor recipe. But the gum-tempera colors, while permanent, will pick up easily when painted over, and at best must be classified as the least effective paint in the tempera family.

EGG TEMPERA

Tempera formulated with the emulsion of egg probably constitutes the earliest known water-soluble medium we will discuss. We know that it has been used effectively since at least 400 A.D. Most of us associate egg tempera with the Renaissance, when it attained enormous popularity, particularly among Italian artists, or with the illuminators of the Middle Ages, who employed egg tempera with incredible beauty and purpose in their religious documents. Usually prepared with the yolk of egg (egg yolk contains its own natural oil), it may also be compounded with both yolk and white, or with the white only. Present-day artists often support the natural egg emulsion with equal measures of various oils and varnishes in order to fortify their colors, yet water always remains the dilutant when working.

Applied to the hard panels generally used with the other tempera paints noted, egg tempera is virtually insoluble when dry and is claimed to be tougher than oil paint. Being a most demanding medium and requiring extreme care and patience, it is not suited for the *alla prima* technique. Because of this limitation, very few of today's painters work with it. Those who do gravitate to this age-old medium find the luminosity and brilliance of color to be irresistible. It would seem ill-advised for those new to painting to become deeply involved with the intricacies of egg tempera, particularly until much further along with their careers.

POSTER COLORS

In my estimation, poster colors are the poorest of the water-base paints. They are essentially *glue* colors, coarsely ground and therefore very opaque, but their main disadvantage is that the undercolor will pick up very easily and alter any overpainting. This bleeding is disturbing to the artist, especially when he attemps to change a hue. Poster colors are very susceptible to damage by the slightest moisture exposure, and will crack or chip if applied too thickly. These colors are quite properly suited to classroom and commercial purposes.

SYNTHETIC PAINTS

The synthetics or plastics are considered by many artists to be the paints of the future, and there is no question that they have been gaining popularity with artists throughout the world. These versatile colors were born in the chemist's laboratory and are likely to prove the most durable of all paints. Synthetics are highly sophisticated colors that are marketed under myriad titles and trade names, but all are very similar in manipulation and character. While no one paint can ever completely supplant another with respect to behavior or result, the range of the synthetics knows no boundaries; for example, they may be applied equally well in delicate wash or heavy impasto. Obviously such combinations of diverse qualities lead to scintillating and inimitable results.

The completed statement in synthetic will more often than not resemble an oil painting. The quickness of drying plus the infinite ease with which corrections or changes may be made remain the primary reasons for the growing popularity of the synthetics. Still there are numerous other advantages, such as the development of a very effective modeling paste. This material is essentially a combination of polymer emulsion and marble dust and may be applied to the support or mixed into the color. It has excellent adhering ability and may be shaped, carved or chiseled, thus affording the painter exceptional latitude in the area of surface relief.

Additionally, synthetics are available in extremely brilliant hues, and have proved to be tough, durable, and permanent. When they were first marketed there was some complaint about their consistency or workability, but this has been corrected.

The bulk of manufactured synthetic paint to be found on the shelves of artists' supply houses are commonly referred to as acrylics. Most labels carry three words, *acrylic polymer emulsion*, are sold under various trade names, and are non-toxic. Polymer medium may be used for mixing, glazing, and even fixing collage. It is also used to prepare a highly sophisticated tempera paint. The ease with which the artist may prepare his own tempera to fit his own needs is unbelievable: one need only grind dry pigment in a minimum amount of water and add the polymer medium.

Synthetics, as well as all modern plastic materials, are created through the process of polymerization. To fully describe this complex process would be too digressive for our purpose, but if you will visualize molecules fused or joined to form larger groups (through catalytic action), you will have witnessed polymerization. Or another way fully to appreciate the phenomenal nature of this new and exciting paint would be to apply a layer over a slightly oily surface and then peel it off when dry. It will have fused itself into a powerful thickness of color, very tough yet highly flexible. When applied properly to clean, non-oily surfaces that have been suitably prepared, acrylic will adhere with tenacity to wood, canvas (primed or not), metal, Masonite, hardboard, paperboard, paper, and even masonry.

Curiously enough, with all of the qualities listed above, many artists react unfavorably to the speed with which acrylics dry. They find that there is not time enough to *work* the paint. So manufacturers, always alert to artists' reactions, have been quick to respond. They have come up with a preparation to retard drying which is nothing more than a traditional glycerin-based recipe used in watercolor for many years. It is altogether possible that the synthetics will in time become the most universally accepted paint in the history of art.

The pictorial statement to follow will include some of the media discussed above, plus other inventive combinations. The attempt here will be to examine retrospectively the event of the painting. With the aid of enlarged sections, you will be able to determine differences that would otherwise be impossible to observe — differences in both artistic temperament and method. You may furthermore detect the artist's enthusiasm and his affection for his work as he senses it growing to completion. While all such thoughts are nothing more than imaginary visions woven with an occasional educated guess, they do prove illuminating and rewarding.

Most artists care little for this kind of autopsy, yet we are inquisitive and eager to learn. It is in this spirit alone that the essay is offered. It is hoped that through patient examination of each painting, new avenues of personal exploration will await the viewer.

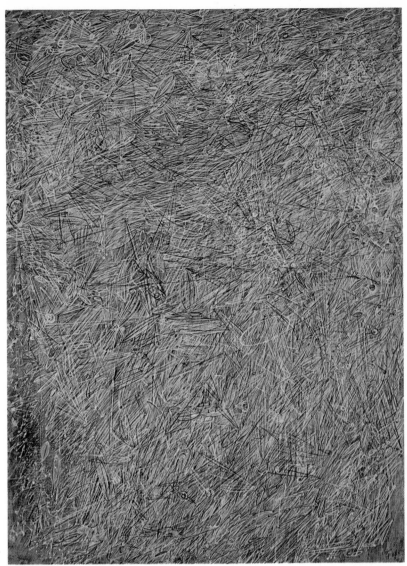

The Drift of Summer by Mark Tobey (b. 1890). 1942. Tempera. 28 x 22 inches.

Mark Tobey once stated, "My imagination, it would seem, has its own geography." In the magnificent *Drift of Summer* one is transported on an exclusive tour over a part of that geography.

Tobey has been referred to as a spiritualist, symbolist, and mystic. It is significant that work of such deeply philosophical nature is also technically flawless. Artist and medium are inexorably welded, thus eliminating mechanical procedures and allowing accident and discovery to follow. The detail reveals the striking patterns formed by multitudes of crossing lines that flood the surface. Because of the translucent quality of tempera, the work inherits soft, persuasive depth-layers, which add to its intrigue. Tobey's work of this period has been called "white line" or "light line": however we choose to describe it, the fluidity of his brush is enchanting.

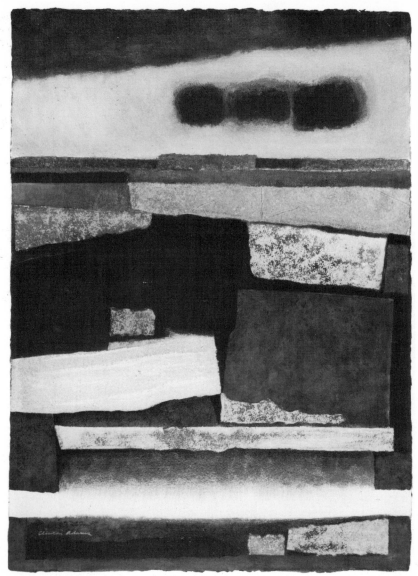

Desert Landscape by Clinton Adams (b. 1918). 1960. Polymer tempera, collage on paper. 30 x 22 inches.

Discriminating selection has always been a characteristic of Clinton Adams' work. Here we find a notable example of his care, restraint, and ultimate victory in reducing desert elements to their simplest terminology.

When first viewing *Desert Landscape,* we see merely flattened shapes, floating, superimposed, and butting against one another. Massive earth-layers play against a distant sky, and we feel the eerie tranquility of the Western desert. But like the desert itself, this painting offers much more to the patient observer, as one suspects after careful examination of the underground labyrinth.

Through the magic of enlargement all suspicions are confirmed. Patterns, textures, and movements of unusual complexion hint of deeper life. Clinton Adams truly develops an unparalleled synthesis of media and content in this exquisite painting.

COURTESY OF THE PASADENA ART MUSEUM. PHOTO I. SERISAWA.

Automaton by Karl Zerbe (b. 1903). 1955. Gouache and collage on canvas. 48 x 24 inches.

No artist could better serve the purpose of this section than the deliberate experimentalist, Karl Zerbe. Widely acclaimed for his monumental achievements in encaustic, he shows here another facet of his *ouevre* with a most eventful combination of translucent gouache with collage.

Automaton is a powerful statement which presents man's inner self as a microcosm of our chaotic world. Elaborately formed and infinitely complex, it demands more than one viewing. The collage includes mysterious numbers and letters. Undercolors peek through from beneath a resist-like layer; line darts about incisively. The impressive detail exposes a faceted understructure stuck together with a weblike mucilage, and the viewer is caught up in Zerbe's frightening self-examination.

COLLECTION OF MR. AND MRS. ROBERT A. ROWAN.

Winged Hue by Morris Louis (1912-1962). 1959. Acrylic resin paint on canvas (mixed media). 96 x 96 inches.

Nowhere in the world of contemporary painting do we find more staggering examples of the new plastic-base paint than in the *oeuvre* of Morris Louis. Louis not only employed a special version of Magna color (a paint miscible in water or turpentine), but added a great deal more of

the original medium (acrylic resin) in order to thin his paint further. In this we discover a specific kinship between Louis and the Oriental masters. Louis, however, continues on to present a mammoth, introspective spectacle, and subject matter is non-existent. His paintings are often referred to as "veils," "drapes," or "florals," and *Winged Hue* is indeed well described by the last term.

While some artists, such as Tobey, re-

ject intense color, and still others abandon line, Louis's work may be devoted to either or both at various times. The impression of a microcosmic world enlarged to extraordinary proportions overwhelms the viewer standing before a Louis painting. Never has the sheer beauty of transparent wash been so eloquently presented; apropos, the detail has been omitted in order to present *Winged Hue* as large as possible.

Country Landscape by Sam Amato (b. 1924). 1967. Acrylic. 96 x 96 inches.

My recent work has been directed to a wide range of pictorial experiments — most of them dealing with African landscape with or without animals as subject matter. I've been leaning-out my paint (acrylic), until it almost resembles watercolor, which I modulate by the use of successive wash-glazes and small marks. My drawing and feeling for light have been directed increasingly toward photographic objectivity, although poetic motivations are my principal determinants in working through a painting.

Sam Amato's words sum up precisely how the artist becomes involved with considerations of media, subject, and poetry. His concern for light alone demands dramatic alterations of paint consistency. By thinning his paint he not only gains light effects through glazing, but also is able to manipulate his paint more quickly and give fuller attention to his poetic goals.

Untitled #1 by Gordon Wagner (b. 1915). 1966. Collage, mixed media. 22 x 30 inches.

One might easily read philosophical meanings into this provocative statement by Gordon Wagner, but our purpose is to examine the dynamics of the work. We look to its revelation of fragments and glimpses of the artist's own world, a world filled with vigorous contrasts of patterns, textures, shapes, and scale.

The detail further intrigues us not only with the physical dimension of collage, but an even more imposing illusion of varied elements floating through space. This invites one to return to the painting with more anticipation than before.

At work here is an elusive bilateral symmetry that is managed with extreme care. One may, through the persuasion of letters and words, sense a billboarded wall, but an infinite space takes bold issue with this interpretation.

Boy with Kites by John Kwok (b. 1920). 1959. Casein. 19 x 28 inches.

John Kwok's paintings have been widely acclaimed for their incisive yet tender poetry. While his recent work has properly turned in new directions, *Boy with Kites* remains a characteristically compassionate statement, masterfully executed.

Casein paint, essentially translucent, may range from full transparency to opacity with ease. The very nature of the paint not only allows this, but offers its own dividends along the way. Kwok displays here a brilliant use of the inimitable qualities of casein. He feels no concern for the convention of *fat over lean,* or any other technical restriction. Underwashes are followed by countless overbrushings and still more washes, which now essentially become glazes: this provides the vibrant character of casein painting.

131

The Revolving World by Kenneth Callahan (b. 1906). 1962. Gouache on paper. 14⅛ x 18½ inches.

In this superb statement, as in Tobey's *The Drift of Summer* (page 125), we find the *private journey* to be dominant. The articulate use of gouache encourages a remarkable calligraphy to coalesce with the massive underlying washes. In this way *The Revolving World* gains an enormous sense of scale, yet it is a relatively small painting.

Kenneth Callahan's use of watercolor has been influenced by the Oriental, without an attempt to adopt its methods. The detail shows the extent to which Callahan is at ease with all facets of his medium, for the intricate and indescribable manipulations so evident in the enlargement properly play a supporting but minor role in the total drama.

The theme is Christ's crucifixion as the hub of a chaotic whirling of animals, people, planets, etc. This painting is but one of many works devoted to the role of man in the cosmic scheme. One never feels that he has absorbed all that exists within the confines of Callahan's margins.

132

Nature's Abyss by Alexander Nepote (b. 1913). 1967. Watercolor, acrylic, and collage on Masonite.

No more unusual experimentation is shown on these pages than this painting by Alexander Nepote, for here is an artist who, in his own words, relies upon "99 percent straight transparent watercolor and a little acrylic." But this is only part of the story.

In the handsome *Nature's Abyss,* the artist's sense of the dramatic seizes and challenges the viewer, confronting him with the overpowering weight and dynamic energy of natural forces.

In surveying the detail it is difficult to believe that one is viewing a painting executed on a flat ground. The dimensional layers present their own peculiar surface variations and seem to be carved out in a more lithic or bas-relief manner.

COURTESY KRAMER GALLERY. PHOTO VIRGINIA MC INTIRE.

133

134

APPENDIX

Two Nude Females by Auguste Rodin.
1900-1905. Pencil and brown watercolor
wash on light gray paper. 7¾ x 12 inches.

MATERIALS AND EQUIPMENT

It may seem incongruous in such a treatise as this to concern ourselves with materials and equipment. However, even though the best of these things cannot do the work for the artist, there are specific advantages inherent in manufactured products that are worthy of our attention. Here again it seems imperative to stress the fact that this knowledge is vital only in allowing the artist fulfillment in attaining esthetic or content goals. He must know what to expect of his materials in performance and durability, and he must also know what to seek out in brush, paint, and support. Furthermore, such advice need in no way inhibit or restrict the artists' deep concern for expressive freedom; instead, proper materials assist sound craftsmanship and join to preserve the art legacy. It is deplorable that some contemporary painters seem contemptuous when the future of art is involved; yet these same artists are extremely dependent upon the heritage which has survived for centuries. Whether such attitudes spring from an anti-art doctrine or are simply the results of bitterness or haplessness is irrelevant. The fact remains that knowingly to produce faulty work is highly unethical. It is of little comfort that the business ethic in today's world condones the principle of built-in obsolescence.

There is intent upon my part to make this section as brief as possible, while still attempting to be thorough. The best explanation for this summary treatment is not the inability to provide the typical photographs and diagrams of artists' equipment, but instead to accord such concerns only a properly proportioned emphasis. There is little question that *one afternoon* spent in any well-stocked art store would result in a more effective knowledge of materials than reading about or gazing at photographs of them. The subjective responses to touch, weight, size, color, and even aroma will play a role in this delightful affair. Should you be fortunate enough to find responsible, informed men working in your art-supply shop, you may rely upon their knowledge of materials and good advice in framing. How to present or frame work is not a subject consistent with the goals of this treatise, but one can hardly underestimate the ultimate importance of such things. Many distinguished artists are by their own admission highly incompetent in this area and depend entirely upon their framers. The common fault in framing is usually that of creating unnecessary interest in the frame itself, which in turn detracts from the painting. Or in simple language, too many paintings suffer from being overframed.

To return to the subject of materials — and on the lighter side — wherever or whenever artists congregate, animated discussions range from philosophical attitudes to a newly marketed paint. What is the nature of the paint, its consistency, its stubbornness or pliability, the drying factor, and with the newer products in particular, the omnipresent question of volatility and toxicity? The textures and aromas of artists' materials are unique and often delightful. My initial encounters with gum and kneaded erasers still remain in my memory. The thrill of my first decent

brush and the feel of it in my hands was eventful. The names of colors piqued my imagination. My first bicycle was repainted in Chinese vermilion. Van Dyke brown was never guaranteed to be permanent, and aureolin yellow twisted most young artists' tongues. Exotic travels were proposed by the use of Persian orange. Pompeian red, French ultramarine blue — the list is endless. There was joy in opening a new can of paint, dipping into it for the first time or squeezing it on the mixing surface. My revered teacher used to state unequivocally, "If you enjoy squeezing toothpaste onto your toothbrush, you'll be a helluva painter." The dedicated artist at any stage of his career will have an inordinate curiosity about his materials and equipment. Furthermore, he will continue to read their every label and brochure completely and investigate every aspect of their composition and habits.

The following text has deep purpose or it would not have been included here. This rather obvious statement is set down to reinforce the belief that, as simple as they may appear, these suggestions have been painstakingly gone over again and again in order to eliminate the superfluous. If nothing more, you should be able to avoid questionable purchases and select materials directly helpful in attaining your goals. It should be kept in mind that in the purchase of artists' materials, as with virtually everything else in our society, the quality items are generally more expensive. Lastly, the ensuing text is devoted exclusively to the materials and equipment of the transparent watercolor medium, for

as you may have determined from reading the descriptions of related water-soluble media (Section 6), the identifying personality of watercolor lies largely in the transparent, translucent or glazed area.

PAINT

The finest transparent watercolors manufactured are not only prepared with the best pigment and binders obtainable, but are expertly formulated and ground. The most versatile of these paints are offered in *tube* containers and are of extremely heavy, syrup-like consistency akin to oil paint. While *cake* or *hard-pan* watercolors may be used successfully by competent painters, they are rarely preferred. The major objections are that they consume valuable time and effort to dilute or soften, and even then the resultant hues are often tinted substitutes of the desired depth or chroma. When the words *Artists Colors* appear on a paint container, this distinguishes the paint from that of the inferior quality of *Student* and *Scholastic* designation. The latter colors are extremely weak by comparison and contain excessive fillers and insufficient pigment. As noted with the pan watercolors, full saturation of color is virtually impossible to attain. Student colors are rarely if ever guaranteed to be permanent, and it would be foolhardy to bother with such inferior products.

BRUSHES

Superior watercolor brushes are made from the hair of the sable, and have been meticulously crafted through hand labor. The hairs are shuffled to point inward so that the natural curvature of each individual hair is positioned to create a round, pointed brush. This is mandatory in order to insure that the brush reshape itself even after the most abusive treatment. The better sable brushes are usually set in seamless, nickled ferrules, with at least two or three rings encircling the ferrule. The experienced artist can run his fingers through a brush and immediately determine its quality. A standard test commonly employed at purchase is to dip the brush into water and shake it out vigorously. If the brush snaps back to an erect point it is probably of excellent quality, especially if it lives up to the other requirements of sable and ferrule.

The Japanese brushes we see now and then are delightful to look at and extremely reasonable in price. But it would be far better to leave them in the hands of the Japanese artist who is well aware of how they are to be used. There are times when experimentation with such things may produce stimulating effects, especially in the areas of spontaneous calligraphy and wash. The lamentable fact remains that many American artists haven't the vaguest notion of why the Japanese brush is constructed as it is, or what diligent exercise and training is needed before it may be used with meaning. Conversely the Japanese brush (*fude,* round, and *hake,* flat) is designed for use in a seated position and is to be held vertically; it becomes influential in the tradition and method of Japanese painting. Since the brush is made from the hair of deer, rabbit, badger, sheep, or other animals, it is relatively limp and uncontrollable in unschooled hands.

It is perplexing to note that elementary-school children often paint exquisitely with frightfully inexpensive, worn-out, and flimsy camel's hair brushes. Would they prosper more if finer equipment were available, or would this better remain a mystery? In any event, if the brush is doing what you want it to do, it is the right one; the foregoing comments to the contrary!

There are flat and round brushes in sable and bristle available to the artist in all forms and sizes. Brush catalogs are the most tantalizingly complex inventions known to artists, with a special brush manufactured for every known professional skill. It would be well to remember that in the selection of small brushes it is sensible to acquire the very best for better control, whereas one need not be quite so concerned with the quality level when purchasing larger sizes. The larger round sable brushes are terribly expensive; so much so that many artists resort to the use of the relatively inexpensive flat variety.

PALETTES

Any mixing surface or palette that is impervious to water is suitable for watercolor paint. A white metal surface is highly desirable because it is unbreakable and one may visualize color mixtures readily. If the mixing surface is porous, the liquid components of your paint will be absorbed into the palette and your color will be unfit for proper use. Since the vast majority of watercolor supports are white, one may readily appreciate the advantages of a white palette. If the palette has small bins around the mixing areas to house the squeezed-out paint, it will prove both useful and economical. Unlike oil or the newer acrylics, it is helpful to leave unused watercolor (even if hardened) in the palette bins. When fresh paint is squeezed over the older and relatively hard color the hardened color will soften in short order. Washing off the palette just prior to use serves the double purpose of cleaning the mixing areas and remoistening the hardened colors.

SUPPORTS

Watercolor paper is produced in various textures, weights or thicknesses, and dimensions. A 400-pound paper is far heavier and thicker than a 72-pound paper. All such papers are graded by the weight of the ream. The superior papers are handmade of linen rag, and have been sized with either a glue or gelatin substance. They are tough and durable, and will withstand much abuse. The sizing procedure is designed to keep the applied paint predominantly on the surface, rather than allowing it to sink in as would be the tendency with unsized or blotter-type paper. Naturally, the resultant color is far more vibrant, and reworking the surface becomes a relatively simple procedure. Such reworking is virtually impossible on cheaper watercolor paper or substitutes.

When deviating from paper especially prepared for watercolor, it is necessary to seek out a support that will lend itself to a desired goal. Working on a stretched cotton cloth will prove a rewarding experience. Stimulating results stem from priming your own choice of paper with either a casein, acrylic, or gesso ground. Rice papers as well as any number of drawing papers or commercially prepared boards may be employed with good effect. For over a year my work was executed on a cotton skrim cloth which was originally manufactured to sack potatoes. This material was prepared with a polyethylene backing, which rendered it incapable of buckling or wrinkling when saturated.

The rougher-textured papers will remain damp longer than their smoother counterparts, since the numerous interstices retain pockets of water. When wetness is prolonged, more manipulation is possible, and for this reason the rougher papers are generally preferred. In addition, the rougher surface allows the artist to place the support in a more upright or vertical position, since the wet paint is held in the tiny depressions of the paper and will not run easily. Smoother paper produces other effects and is not as workable, but there remain valid reasons why artists wish to work with the smoother stock from time to time. Working on smoother papers discourages manipulation and in turn exposes the spectacle of brush calligraphy.

The extremely heavy papers of 400-pound weight are actually of board thickness. They do not require stretching as is recommended with the lighter weights from 140-pound on down. Watercolor blocks are offered as stretched paper, but this is erroneous: they are simply glue-bound around the edges and will buckle severely when saturated. Almost all fine watercolor papers can be identified by their embossments or watermarks, which may indicate the preferred side, but most better papers are usable on both sides.

In stretching or preparing your support, the simplest method is to tape or staple the paper down onto a drawing board or a common plywood backing. By wetting both sides or soaking the paper in a tub of water for a minute or two, you allow the paper to expand, and while in this state of expansion, it should be secured to the board. When dry, the paper will have drawn taut through shrinkage and will have become an excellent painting support. Rolling the wet paper in your hands to form a cylinder just prior to spreading it out over the board, will aid in getting it down flat for securing the edges. Use only the gummed-paper tape for this purpose, as the cellulose and masking tapes are not suitable. Neither are any of the pressure-sensitive variety. If stapling, be certain to stay at least a half-inch away from the edges of the paper and keep the staples about two to three inches apart. There are numerous other ways to prepare the watercolor support, but they all serve the same purpose. Some prefer gluing down the edges, while others build complicated rigs that clasp the paper in the manner of embroidery hoops. But rather than dwell on this phase of preparation as a method, let me re-emphasize why such care is important.

Working on a prestretched taut surface virtually eliminates unmanageable buckling. What little swelling may occur (some is inevitable) quickly vanishes as the paper dries. It is difficult to work on anything but a flat surface in any medium, but this is especially so with watercolor. Not only does the artist have to contend with unwanted nuances of light and shadow that result from the uneven surface, but washes have a tendency to form undesirable pools of color in the troughs of the paper. The sooner one dispenses with the physical concerns in painting, the more intimately and vigorously may one then turn to content and meaning.

Some artists frown upon all such procedural advice, and while it is easy to agree with them in spirit, they make little sense. Technological awareness will often lead to a new environment of discovery, but only when it is not offered as a strict rule. It is always the result we are searching for. For example, by saturating a paper and spreading it out unstretched over any non-absorbent surface such as glass, a unique wet-into-wet result is achieved. Placing a blotter under the paper, whether stretched or not, will prolong the drying time of the paper and afford the painter wider manipulative power. Working at night or in a damp, humid climate will cause slower drying, while a hot, dry environment forces paint seemingly to dry upon contact with the paper. Lastly, by varying the weight of the paper, its surface, or composition, countless other qualities are within reach. Experience alone will make the foregoing meaningful and, more importantly, will ultimately beckon you down new avenues of investigation. It would seem to me that no serious painter at work with this elegant medium could afford not to explore its fullest range of dynamic potential.

EASELS

Whether one works in a studio or on location, there is one demand to be considered when acquiring an easel suitable for watercolor. Because of the elusiveness of the wash, it is often desirable to flatten the working surface to a more horizontal position. Therefore, it will prove helpful to employ an easel that not only adjusts vertically but will tilt back to adjust horizontally too. Watercolor easels are manufactured in various sizes and weights and are fabricated out of every known material. It is far more sensible to select a durable product that may be used indoors and out (therefore, too, it should be collapsible and transportable). The flimsy, light-weight items should be avoided. Any additional cost in purchasing a quality easel proves negligible in the long run, and will repeatedly spare your time and energy.

Watercolor is a medium which, by its nature, allows the artist to function day or night, in studio or on location, and during fair or foul weather. Because of the speed with which expression is gained (especially under adverse conditions), it is all the more important to be well prepared. This is evident in the note-taking area, where watercolor has long been relied upon as a means of gathering relatively complete information. Remember that Turner's sketches are now considered by many to be his major contribution and that Homer always rated his efforts in watercolor to be of greater importance than his oils.

Artists' supply houses offer such things as miniature palettes, collapsible water containers, and quaint brushes that break in half to fit the minute palette. Indeed, all of this equipment fits neatly into a shirt pocket. There was a time when this dilettantish material used to amuse me, but not for long. In years to follow, this miniature equipment was invaluable to me when, as an artist-correspondent during World War II, I was forced to work in tight quarters on assignment, backstage, etc. While my purposes then were mainly reference-oriented, and the results were of a very intimate nature, there is little doubt in my mind that this work could not have been produced in any other way.

May I repeat that whatever is offered here is only a suggestion based upon what we now know of contemporary materials and equipment. This has been drawn from personal experience and under no circumstances can be considered complete. It may be a starting point for many, as it has been for me. It may provide a reinforcement to promote confidence, sureness, and belief. It may, in the interim, save you time and expense, while sparing your energies as you struggle for expression.

BIBLIOGRAPHY

Albers, Joseph. *Interaction of Color.* New Haven: Yale University Press, 1963.

Arnheim, Rudolph. *Art and Visual Perception.* Berkeley: University of California Press, 1954.

Barr, Alfred H. Jr. (ed.). *Cubism and Abstract Art.* New York: The Museum of Modern Art, 1936.

————. *Fantastic Art Dada Surrealism.* New York: The Museum of Modern Art, 1936.

————. *Masters of Modern Art.* New York: The Museum of Modern Art, 1954.

Beazly, Sir John. *Masterpieces of Greek Drawing and Painting.* New York: Macmillan, 1955.

Butlin, Martin. *Turner Watercolours.* New York: Watson-Guptill, 1965.

Calderon, W. Frank. *Animal Painting and Anatomy.* Philadelphia: Lippincott (n.d.).

Cary, Joyce. *Art and Reality.* New York: Anchor Books, Doubleday, 1961.

Doerner, Max. *The Materials of the Artist.* (Rev. ed.). New York: Harcourt, Brace & World, 1949.

Gardner, Helen. *Art Through the Ages.* New York: Harcourt, Brace & World, 1959.

Goodrich, Lloyd. *Winslow Homer.* New York: Macmillan, 1944.

Graziosi, Paolo. *Palaeolithic Art.* New York: McGraw-Hill, 1960.

Grosz, George. *Ecce Homo.* Introduction by Henry Miller. New York: Grove Press, 1966.

Hambidge, Jay. *The Elements of Dynamic Symmetry.* New York: Dover, (n.d.).

Helm, MacKinley. *John Marin.* Boston: Pellegrini and Cudahay, 1948.

Heron, Patrick. *The Changing Forms of Art.* New York: The Noonday Press, 1958.

Itten, Johannes. *The Art of Color.* New York: Reinhold Book Corp., 1961.

Janson, H. W. *History of Art.* New York: Harry N. Abrams, 1962.

Jensen, Lawrence N. *Synthetic Painting Media.* Englewood Cliffs, New Jersey: Prentice-Hall, 1964.

Johnson, Una E. *Drawings of the Masters: 20th Century Drawings.* Parts I and II. New York: Shorewood Publishers, 1964.

Kandinsky, Wassily. *Concerning the Spiritual in Art & Painting in Particular.* New York: Wittenborn, 1964.

Kepes, Gyorgy. *Language of Vision.* Chicago: Theobald, 1945.

Klee, Paul. *Pedagogical Sketchbook.* New York: Frederick A. Praeger, 1953.

Lebrun, Rico. *Rico Lebrun Drawings.* Berkeley & Los Angeles: University of California Press, 1961.

Loran, Erle. *Cézanne's Composition* (3rd ed.). Berkeley: University of California Press, 1963.

Malraux, André. *The Voices of Silence.* New York: Doubleday, 1953.

Mayer, Ralph. *The Artist's Handbook.* (Rev. ed.). New York: The Viking Press, 1957.

Mekhitarian, Arpag. *Egyptian Painting.* Translated by Stuart Gilbert. New York: Skira, 1954.

Mitsch, Erwin. *Egon Schiele.* Salzburg: Verlag Galerie Welz, 1961.

Nicolaides, Kimon. *The Natural Way to Draw.* Boston: Houghton Mifflin, 1941.

Pallottino, Massimo. *Etruscan Painting.* New York: Skira, 1953.

Rasmusen, Henry. *Art Structure.* New York: McGraw-Hill, 1950.

Read, Herbert. *A Concise History of Modern Painting.* New York: Frederick A. Praeger, 1959.

Rewald, John. *The History of Impressionism.* (Rev. ed.). New York: The Museum of Modern Art, 1962.

Rhys, Hedley Howell. *Maurice Prendergast.* Cambridge: Harvard University Press, 1960.

Ritchie, Andrew C. *Charles Demuth.* New York: The Museum of Modern Art, 1950.

Sachs, Paul J. *Modern Prints and Drawings.* New York: Alfred A. Knopf, 1954.

Selz, Peter. *German Expressionist Painting.* Berkeley: University of California Press, 1957.

Shahn, Ben. *The Shape of Content.* New York: Vintage Books, 1960.

Sweeney, James Johnson. *Henry Moore.* New York: The Museum of Modern Art, 1947.

Taylor, Harold. *Art and the Intellect.* New York: The Museum of Modern Art, 1960.

Taylor, Joshua C. *Learning to Look.* Chicago: The University of Chicago Press, 1957.

Toda, Kenji. *Japanese Scroll Painting.* Chicago: The University of Chicago Press, 1935.

Yashiro, Yukio. *2,000 Years of Japanese Art.* New York: Harry N. Abrams, 1958.

INDEX

A (Altoon), 51
Action painting, 62
Adams, Clinton, 126
Albers, Josef, 44, 45
Albright, Ivan, 100
Alla prima painting, 14, 81, 120, 122
Allegory (Callahan), 118
Altoon, John, 51
Amato, Sam, 129
American school, 16-17, 30-31, 37
Anatomy, study of, 43
An Ancient Beech Tree (Sandby), 26
Ancient Grass (Olson), 87
Architectural form, 43
Arcimboldo, Giuseppe, 61, 62
Armory Show (1913), 36, 61
Arp, Hans, 62
The Artist's Approach to the New Nature
    (Brigante), 65
Austrian expressionism, 35
Automaton (Zerbe), 127
The Bank (Reep), 98, 106
Bathing Women (Dufy), 33
Bauhaus school, 34, 36, 100
Beach (Kramer), 90
The Beach (Reep), 108, 109
Bettencourt, Pierre, 55
Bezold, Wilhelm von, 45
Bird (Graves), 85
Bisttram, E. J., 101, 105
Blake, William, 16, 28
Bluemner, Oscar Florianus, 35
Bonnard, Pierre, 43, 60
Bosch, Hieronymus, 60, 61
Boy with Kites (Kwok), 131
Bradshaw, Glen R., 71
Brazil, Maurice, 31
Brigante, Nick, 65, 93
British school, 16, 25-29
Brush Drawing (Kling), 78
Brushes, 137-138
Burchfield, Charles, 17, 37, 62
Byzantine mosaics, 16
Callahan, Kenneth, 118, 132
Casein tempera, 121
Cave painting, 13, 18-19
    See also Lascaux Cave
Cézanne, Paul, 17, 52, 60
Chevreul, Michel, 45
Chinese scrolls, 22
The City (Man and Woman), (Grosz),
    49

Clear Weather in the Valley (Tung
    Yüan), 22
Clifford, Henry, 40
Collage, 111
Color, 44-45
Color physics, 44
Composition, 41-43
Composition (Nay), 57, 66
Country Landscape (Amato), 129
Cross, Watson, 67, 101
Crown, Keith, 54, 56, 57, 72
Crystalware in Brown (Reep), 109, 112
Crystalware in Pink (Reep), 109
Cubism, 41, 60-61
Cutrow, Leonard, 69, 95
Dadaists, 61
Daumier, Honoré, 29
Da Vinci, Leonardo, 38, 43
Day in Echo Park (Reep), 108, 109
Davies, Arthur B., 17
Delacroix, Eugène, 29
Delaunay, Robert, 60
Demaphon #2 (Cutrow), 95
Demuth, Charles, 17, 50
Der Blaue Reiter, 60
Desert Landscape (Adams), 126
Die Brücke, 60
Distortion, 41
Divisionism, 60
Draftsmanship, 42-43, 46
Dragonade (Tobey), 58
Drawings (Lebrun), 46
Dream (Edmondson), 68
The Drift of Summer (Tobey), 125, 132
Dubuffet, Jean, 54, 55
Duchamp, Marcel, 61
Dufy, Raoul, 33
Dürer, Albrecht, 16, 24
Dynamic Symmetry, 42, 101, 105
Easels, 139
Ecce Homo (Grosz), 49
Edmondson, Leonard, 68, 96
Egg tempera, 122-123
Egyptian painting, 15, 20
English school. *See* British school
Ensor, James, 60
Ernst, Max, 62
Esthetics, primitive, 19
Etruscan painting, motif, 15
Euclid, 42
Euphony (Reep), 112, 113
Evening Star, III (O'Keeffe), 84

Expressionism. *See* specific schools or
    countries
Fantasy, as theme, 16
Far Eastern schools, 13
Fauves, 32, 33, 60
Feininger, Lyonel, 17, 36
Figure with Bandaged Legs (Lebrun), 46
Flowers Cyclamen (Demuth), 50
Formulations (Levy), 94
Francis, Sam, 54, 62
French Impressionists, 17
Frescoes, Middle Ages, 16
Friezes. *See* cave painting, tomb painting
Fugue in the Silence (Levy), 64
Futurism, 61
Garden of Worldly Delights (Bosch), 60
Gauguin, Paul, 60
German Expressionists, 17, 60
Giacometti, Alberto, 40, 70
Goethe, 45
Golden Section, 42
Graham, Donald, 101
Graves, Morris, 84, 85
Gris, Juan, 61
Grosz, George, 49
Group of Three Girls (Schiele), 48
Grouping (Koch), 88
Hambidge, Jay, 101
Happenings, 62
Higgins, Olga, 75
Hokusai, Katsushika, 8
Hölzel, Adolf, 45
Homer, Winslow, 16-17, 30, 59
Horizontal Still-Life (Rebert), 92
Impressionism, 44, 60
    See also French Impressionists
The Inward Sun (Warner), 74
Itten, Johannes, 45
Jamnitzer, Wenzel, 61
Japanese scrolls, 14, 23
Japanese painting, 14
Japanese printmakers, 60
Jardin Nacre (Dubuffet), 55
Jepson, Herbert, 101
Kandinsky, Wassily, 17, 34, 40, 41
Kanemitsu, Matsumi, 89
Khotsa Cave painting (Basutoland), 18,
    19
Kinetics, 17, 103
Klee, Paul, 17, 34-35
Klimt, Gustav, 48
Kling, Jack, 70, 78

Koch, Irene, 88
Kramer, Harold M., 72, 73, 90, 101
Kwok, John, 131
Land, Jerome, 97
Larmessin, 62
Lascaux Cave painting, 18
Leavitt, Dr. Thomas W., 119
Lebrun, Rico, 46
Leger, Fernand, 60
Levy, Hilda, 64, 65, 94
Long Beach Pike (Reep), 104
Lorrain, Claude, 25, 26, 27
Louis, Morris, 128
Low Tide, Beachmont (Brazil), 31
Luminism, 62
Magritte, René, 62
Malibu Series (Kling), 70
Man Reading in a Garden (Daumier), 29
Mantled Shore (Bradshaw), 71
Marin, John, 17, 36, 52-53, 59, 61, 62, 81
Marsh, Reginald, 100
Masson, André, 62
Materials, 45
Matisse, Henri, 32, 33, 40, 44, 60
Mayer, Ralph, 80
McIvor, John W., 76, 77, 91
Message to Paul Klee (Higgins), 75
Methodology, 79-83
Mid-Manhatten (Feininger), 36
Middle Ages, frescoes, 15-16
Miró, Joan, 62
The Mirror (Reep), 86
Modersohn-Becker, Paula, 60
Monet, Claude, 60
Moon Story (Reep), 105
Moore, Henry, 47, 83
Moore, William, 101
Mueller, Otto, 60
Mountain (Reep), 108, 109
Munsell system, 45
Nassau (Homer), 30
Nature's Abyss (Nepote), 133
Nay, Ernst Wilhelm, 54, 56, 57, 66
Nepote, Alexander, 77, 133
Nicolaides, Kimon, 79
Nolde, Emil, 17, 60
Note (Reep), 106
Nude Descending a Staircase (Duchamp), 61
Nude Female Reclining (Schiele), 35
O'Keeffe, Georgia, 62, 84
Olson, Meredith, 87
On Morse Mountain, Small Point, Maine (Marin), 53
1,000 Watercolor Touches (McIvor), 91
Op art, 62
Oracle (Cutrow), 69
Ostwald system, 45
Page from Shelter Sketchbook (Moore), 83
Paint, 137
Palettes, 138

Pan American Exposition Exhibition (Buffalo), 17
Pechstein, Max, 60
Pedagogical Sketchbook (Klee), 34
Perspective, 41-42
Phillips, Thomas, 26
Picabia, Francis, 60
Picasso, Pablo, 46, 117
A Pier Goes On and On (Reep), 104
Pigment, 44-45
Pipe Dream (Reep), 63
Pissarro, Camille, 60
Planes, 41
Pointillists, 60
Pollock, Jackson, 62
Pop art, 62
Post-Impressionism, 60
Poster Colors, 123
Prendergast, Maurice, 17, 31, 33, 59
Primitive art, motif, 19
Psychedelic art, 62
Rebirth (Reep), 102, 103
Red Horses (Kramer), 73
The Red Tear Drop (Edmondson), 96
Reductive art, 62
Reep, Edward, 63, 86, 98-116
Religious themes, 16
Rembrandt van Ryn, 16, 25
Renaissance, watercolor in, 16
Return to the Earth (Reep), 106, 107, 116
The Revolving World (Callahan), 132
River at the Bridge of Trois Sautets (Cézanne), 52
Rivera, Diego, 81
Rodin, Auguste, 6, 134
Roman painting, motif, 15
Rouault, Georges, 32
St. Peter's Port and Castle Cornett (Phillips), 26
Sandby, Paul, 16, 26
Sargent, John Singer, 31
Schiele, Egon, 35, 48
Schwitters, Kurt, 61
Sea and White Lines (Crown), 57
Seascape (Marin), 36
Second Theme with a Double Subject (McIvor), 76
Seurat, Georges, 60, 61
The Shell Heap (Homer), 30
Ship and Cutter (Turner), 27
Shoot First (Reep), 114, 115
Simplon Pass, Avalanche Track (Sargent), 31
Simultaneity, in Cubism, 61
Siporin, Mitchell, 100
6 P.M. Glow, June (Brigante), 93
Sleeping Women (Moore), 47
Slope of a Hill (Delacroix), 29
South Side (Land), 97
Space, 42
Stairway to Yesterday (Reep), 116
Standing Nude (Rodin), 6

Stieglitz, Alfred, 61
Still-Life with Apple #1 (Reep), 105
Studio per la Battaglia di Anghiari, Venice Academy (da Vinci), 38
Subaqueous (Reep), 112
Sumi e painting (Wakeshima), 12
Sumi e painting, 14
Sun Horizon #1 (Reep), 112, 115
Sun Horizon #2 (Reep), 112, 115
Sun and Rocks (Burchfield), 37
Sun Storm (Bluemner), 35
Supports, 138-139
Surrealism, 61-62
Swamp Note (Reep), 102
Symmetry, 42
Synthetic paints, 123-124
Tanguy, Yves, 62
Taylor, Harold, 9
Technique, 79-83
Tempera painting, 14-15, 121
Theban tomb painting, 20
Tiepolo, 16
A Theatrical Character (Hokusai), 8
Three P.M. Fog (Brigante), 64
Le Tibre en Amont de Rome (Lorrain), 25
Tobey, Mark, 58, 62, 125, 128
Tomb of the Old Man, Italy (Etruscan), 21
Tomb paintings, 15, 20, 21
See also Cave paintings
Turner, J.M.W., 16, 27, 28
Tung Yüan, 22
Twittering Machine (Klee), 34, 35
Two Nude Females (Rodin), 134
Two Prostitutes (Rouault), 32
Untitled (Cross), 67
Untitled (Francis), 54
Untitled (Kanemitsu), 89
Untitled #1 (Wagner), 130
Utah Red Cliff (Nepote), 77
Van Gogh, Vincent, 60
View of Arco (Dürer), 24
View of London (Rembrandt), 25
Vuillard, Jean, 43, 60
Wagner, Gordon, 130
Wakeshima, Ken, 12
Warner, Elsa, 74
Wax and gum tempera, 122
The Whirlwind of Lovers (Hell, Canto 5), (Blake), 28
White Line Landscape (Crown), 72
Wind Bouquet (Reep), 106, 107
Windowed Microcosm (Reep), 111
Winged Hue (Louis), 128
World in World (Reep), 110
Yamatoe school, 23
Yang and Yin, 93
Yuzu Nembutsu Engi, 23
Zerbe, Karl, 127